The
Science of Alchemy

**A TREATISE ON THE SCIENCE
OF
SOUL-TRANSMUTATION**

The Text of the Hermetic Sermon on the All and Good entitled "Mind unto Hermes," Together with the Esoteric Commentary, Giving in Full the Esoteric Key to This Great Sermon. The Official Interpretation of the Hermetic Brotherhood of Atlantis.

Dr. A. S. Raleigh

LATE OFFICIAL SCRIBE OF THE
HERMETIC BROTHERHOOD
AND
HIEROPHANT OF THE MYSTERIES OF ISIS

ISBN 1-56459-007-0

Request our FREE CATALOG of over 1,000
Rare Esoteric Books
Unavailable Elsewhere

Alchemy, Ancient Wisdom, Astronomy, Baconian, Eastern-Thought, Egyptology, Esoteric, Freemasonry, Gnosticism, Hermetic, Magic, Metaphysics, Mysticism, Mystery Schools, Mythology, Occult, Philosophy, Psychology, Pyramids, Qabalah, Religions, Rosicrucian, Science, Spiritual, Symbolism, Tarot, Theosophy, *and many more!*

Kessinger Publishing Company
Montana, U.S.A.

CONTENTS

Introductory Note 7

Text 10

Lesson   I. The All and Good.............. 21

Lesson   II. God and Æon 33

Lesson   III. The Æon Lore................. 46

Lesson   IV. Æonology ..,.................. 60

Lesson   V. The Unity of Life............. 78

Lesson   VI. The One Maker of All.......... 90

Lesson   VII. The Divine Workman............105

Lesson   VIII. Life and Death................114

Lesson   IX. The Master's Word.............131

Lesson   X. Æonian Life 145

DEDICATION

To Mrs. Caroline Mesloh through whose assistance it was possible to publish the four Hermetic Works. The Shepherd of Men; Woman and Superwoman; Philosophia Hermetica and Scientifica Hermetica; thereby enabling the world of the present Age to come into possession of the Hermetic Gnosis, something that was not possible without the study of those Text Books in Hermetic Wisdom; in recognition of her faithful co-operation in this work of enlightenment: this Set of Lessons in The Science of Alchemy is lovingly Dedicated.

INTRODUCTORY NOTE

We herewith present to our Students the following Treatise on The Science of Alchemy. It is written to serve two purposes: first, it gives the Text of the Sermon of Mind to Hermes on the Nature of the All and Good, and contains the Official Esoteric Commentary of the Hermetic Brotherhood of Atlantis; in the second place, it will be found to be the Official Text Book of the Brotherhood, for students of the Science of Alchemy. These Lessons will be found to unfold the fundamental principles of the Science of Alchemy, and of the nature of Eternal Life in a way that will be most easily understood by the student.

In the Ninth and Tenth Lessons the most important instruction will be found. It is there that the work becomes practical. In those two Lessons are given Nine of the Thirteen Hermetic Disciplines for the consummation of the Great Work of Soul Transmutation. Here you will find the Secret of Self-immortalization clearly revealed to you. Here it is shown that the real Magic is merely the Magical Power of Thought. We learn that man is exactly what he thinks, and that He is the absolute Master of his Destiny simply by using the thought of his own mind as the means of transforming himself into that which he wishes to be. The Path outlined here is the Path of Knowledge, of Thought and of Power. It is shown that man must save himself, and that it is through thought that he accomplishes this result. There are Thirteen Hermetic Disciplines, through which this Transmutation of Soul and Life is brought about; by which a man becomes Æonian or Eternal rather than merely Immortal, and we are here given Nine of the Thirteen Disciplines. As all the transmutation is accomplished through the action of Thought, as it is the Mind that does this work, it is most important that we should have a mind trained to think in the correct manner, a disciplined mind in fact. The purpose of the Hermetic Discipline is the disciplining of the mind. We do not try to discipline the will, or the conduct, but only the mind, that it may think correctly, in which case we are bound to attain perfection. It is for this reason that it is so essential that the mind should be disciplined, and when all of the Thirteen Disciplines are applied, the mind will be perfectly disciplined, and will therefore, be the instrument of the perfecting of Godhood in yourself.

The Nine Disciplines that we give in these Lessons are as follows: In the First Discipline you must train the mind to think of the bodiless. Train it to think of things apart from size, weight, body and form; to think of them independent of the three Dimensions of length, breadth and thickness; to think of all things in their Fourth Dimension. In the Second Discipline, which can only be applied after the first one has been mastered; you must learn to think from yourself; that is, think without objects to suggest thought, think objectively rather than subjectively; generate your thought in the mind without any outside assistance. When this has been mastered, you are now ready to undertake the Third Discipline. This is through the action of thought to cause your soul to be in places other than that in which your body is located at the time; to completely master this exercise, so that you can be instantly in whatever place you think about is to master the Third Discipline. Now, you are ready to undertake the Fourth Discipline. This is on the same order as the Third Discipline, though it is carried to a much greater height than in the Third Discipline. In this Discipline the Soul must master the entire Cosmos in the same way that it did the Earth in the Third Discipline, it must become omnipresent throughout the entire Cosmos, and even expand until it is able to go beyond the Cosmos, and in fact be present in all parts of the Cosmos and even in Extra-Cosmic Space as well. The Fifth Discipline is that by which you learn to hold all things in your mind as thoughts, so that there is nothing that is not present in your mind as a thought. In the Sixth Discipline you not only contain within yourself, all bodies as thoughts but likewise all souls, you contain Time in your mind as a thought, and transcending Time, you contain the Intelligible Cosmos in your Mind as a thought, and not only that, but Eternity, that is Æon is likewise present in your mind as thought. Now you are ready for the Seventh Discipline; this is accomplished by conceiving yourself as possessed of all power so that nothing is impossible unto you, thinking yourself deathless, and possessed of all knowledge, visualizing all arts, all sciences and the way of every life within your own mind, so that you become conscious of all these things, and thus know them as being parts of your own consciousness. The Eighth Discipline is accomplished by imaging in your mind as thought every possible condition of life, every possible experience of every force in nature, every element and every creature, so that they are all within you, and you possess within you the sensations and consciousness of every thing and every life. The Ninth Discipline is accomplished when you reach the point where you are all of these things and conditions at once, all times, all places, all doings, all qualities, all quantities, transcending all time as well as all space, being everything past, present and future, unto Infinity, and this all as simultaneous consciousness. When you have mastered this Discipline all this is within the possession of your mind and is there as thought. The other Four Disciplines belong to the Practical Art of Alchemy, and so will not be given here as they are not treated in this Set of Lessons. You will find in these Lessons all that you need to make you a perfect Master of the Science of Alchemy.

A. S. RALEIGH.

Berros, Calif., March 15, 1918.

THE SCIENCE OF ALCHEMY

Mind Unto Hermes

Text

Parthey (G.) *Hermetis Trismegisti Poemander* (Berlin, 1854), 85-93.

Patrizzi (F.) *Nova de Universis Philosophia* (Venice, 1593), 20b-23.

Mead (G. R. S.) *Thrice Greatest Hermes* (London, 1906). Corpus Hermeticum XI. (XII.)

1. *Mind*. Master this sermon *(logos)*, then, Thrice-greatest Hermes, and bear in mind the spoken words; and as it hath come unto Me to speak, I will no more delay.

Hermes. As many men say many things, and these diverse, about the All and Good, I have not learned the truth. Make it, then, clear to me, O Master mine! For I can trust the explanation of these things, which comes from Thee alone.

2. *Mind*, hear [then], My son, how standeth God and All.

God; Æon; Cosmos; Time; Becoming.

God maketh Æon; Æon Cosmos; Cosmos, Time; and Time, Becoming.

The good,—the Beautiful, Wisdom, Blessedness,—is essence, as it were, of God, of Æon, Sameness; of Cosmos, Order; of Time, Change; and of Becoming, Life and Death.

The energies of God are Mind and Soul; of Æon, lastingness and deathlessness; of Cosmos, restoration and the opposite thereof;

of Time, increase and decrease; and of Becoming, quality.

Æon is, then, in God; Cosmos, in Æon; in Cosmos, Time; in Time, Becoming.

Æon stands firm round God; Cosmos is moved in Æon; Time hath its limits in the Cosmos; Becoming doth become in Time.

3. The source, therefore, of all is God; their essence, Æon; their matter, Cosmos.

God's power is Æon; Æon's work is Cosmos—which never *hath* become, yet ever *doth* become by Æon.

Therefore will Cosmos never be destroyed, for Æon's indestructible; nor doth a whit of things in Cosmos perish, for Cosmos is enwrapped by Æon round on every side.

Her. But God's Wisdom—what is that?
Mind. The Good and Beautiful, and Blessedness, and Virtue's all, and Æon.

Æon, then, ordereth [Cosmos], imparting deathlessness and lastingness to matter.

4. For its becoming doth depend on Æon, as Æon doth on God. Now Genesis and Time, in Heaven and on the Earth, are of two natures.

In Heaven they are unchangeable and indestructible, but on the Earth they're subject unto change and to destruction.

Further, the Æon's soul is God; the Cosmos' soul is Æon; the Earth's soul, Heaven.

And God's in Mind; and Mind, in Soul; and Soul, in Matter; and all of them through Æon.

But all this Body, in which are all the bodies is full of Soul; and Soul is full of Mind, and [Mind] of God.

It fills it from within, and from without encircles it, making the All to live.

Without, this vast and perfect Life [encircles] Cosmos; within, it fills [it with] all lives; above, in Heaven, continuing in sameness; below, on Earth, changing becoming.

5. And Æon doth preserve this [Cosmos], or by Necessity, or by Foreknowledge, or by Nature, or by whatever else a man supposes or shall suppose. And all is this,—God energizing.

The Energy of God is Power that naught can e'er surpass, a Power with which no one can make comparison of any human thing at all, or any thing divine.

Wherefore, O Hermes, never think that aught of things above or things below is like to God, for thou wilt fall from truth. For naught is like to That which hath no like, and is Alone and One.

And do not ever think that any other can possibly possess His Power; for what apart from Him is there of life, and deathlessness and change of quality? For what else should He make?

God's not inactive, since all things [then] would lack activity; for all are full of God.

But neither in the Cosmos anywhere, nor in aught else, is there inaction. For that "inaction" is a name that cannot be applied to either what doth make or what is made.

6. But all things must be made; both ever made, and also in accordance with the influence of every space.

For He who makes, is in them all; not stablished in some one of them, nor making one thing only, but making all.

For being Power, He energizeth in the things He makes and is not independent of them,—although the things He makes are subject to Him.

Now gaze through Me upon the Cosmos that's now subject to thy sight; regard its Beauty carefully,—Body is pure perfection, though one than which there's no more ancient one, ever in prime of Life, and ever-young, nay, rather, in even fuller and yet fuller prime!

7. Behold, again, the seven subject Worlds; ordered by Æon's order, and with their varied course full-filling Æon!

[See how] all things [are] full of light, and nowhere [is there] fire; for 'tis the love and blending of the contraries and the dissimilars that doth give birth to light down shining by the energy of God, the Father of all good, the Leader of all order, and Ruler of the seven world-orderings!

[Behold] the Moon, forerunner of them all, the instrument of nature, and the transmuter of its lower matter!

[Look at] the Earth set in the midst of All, foundation of the Cosmos Beautiful, feeder and nurse of things on Earth!

And contemplate the multitude of deathless lives, how great it is, and that of lives subject to death; and midway, between both, immortal [lives] and mortal, [see thou] the circling Moon.

8. And all are full of Soul, and all are moved by it, each in its proper way; some [see] how the right [move] not unto left, nor round the Heaven, others around the Earth;

yet the left unto the right; nor the above below, nor the below above.

And that all these are subject unto Genesis, My dearest Hermes, thou hast no longer need to learn of Me. For that they bodies are, have souls, and they are moved.

But 'tis impossible for them to come together into one without some one to bring them [all] together. It must, then, be that such a one as this must be some one who's wholly One.

9. For as the many motions of them [all] are different, and as their bodies are not like, yet has one speed been ordered for them all, it is impossible that there should be two or more makers for them.

For that one single order is not kept among "the many"; but rivalry will follow of the weaker with the stronger, and they will strive.

And if the maker of the lives that suffer change and death, should be another, he would desire to make the deathless ones as well; just as the maker of the deathless ones, [to make the lives] that suffer death.

But come! If there be two,—if Matter's one, and Soul is one, in whose hands would there be the distribution for the making? Again, if both of them have some of it, in whose hands may there be the greater part?

10. But thus conceive it, then; that every living body doth consist of soul and matter, whether [that body be] of an immortal, or a mortal, or an irrational [life].

For that all living bodies are ensouled; whereas, upon the other hand, those that live not, are matter by itself.

And, in like fashion, Soul when in its self is, after its own maker, cause of life; but *the* cause of all life is He who makes the things that cannot die.

Her. How, then, is it that, first, lives subject unto death are other than the deathless ones? And, next, how is it that that Life which knows no death, and maketh deathlessness, doth not make animals immortal?

11. *Mind.* First, that there is some one who does these things, is clear; and, next, that He is also One, is very manifest. For, also, Soul is one, and Life is one, and Matter one.

Her. But who is He?

Mind. Who may it other be than the One God? Whom else should it beseem to put Soul into lives but God alone? One, then, is God.

It would indeed be most ridiculous, if when thou dost confess the Cosmos to be one, Sun one, Moon one, and Godhead one, thou shouldst wish God Himself to be some one or other of a number!

12. All things, therefore, He makes, in many [ways]. And what great thing is it for God to make life, soul, and deathlessness, and change, when thou [thyself] dost do so many things?

For thou dost see, and speak, and hear, and smell, and taste, and touch, and walk, and think, and breathe. And it is not one man who smells, a second one who speaks, a third who touches, another one who tastes, another one who walks, another one who thinks, and [yet] another one who breathes. But *one* is he who doth all these.

And yet no one of these could be apart from God. For just as, shouldst thou cease from these, thou wouldst no longer be a living thing, so also, should God cease from them (a thing not law to say), no longer is He God.

13. For if it hath been shown that no thing can inactive be, how much less God? For if there's aught He doth not make (if it be law to say), He is imperfect. But if He is not only not inactive, but perfect [God], then He doth make all things.

Give thou thyself to Me, My Hermes, for a little while, and thou shalt understand more easily how that God's work is one, in order that all things may be—that are being made, or once have been, or that are going to be made. And *this* is, My Beloved, Life; this is the Beautiful; this is the Good; this, God.

14. And if thou wouldst in practice understand [this work], behold what taketh place with thee desiring to beget. Yet this is not like unto that, for He doth not enjoy.

For that indeed He hath no other one to share in what He works, for working by Himself, He ever is at work, Himself being what he doth. For did He separate Himself from it, all things would [then] collapse, and all must die, Life ceasing.

But if all things are lives, and also Life is one; then, one is God. And, furthermore, if all are lives, both those in Heaven and those on Earth, and One Life in them all is made to be by God, and God is it—then, all are made by God.

Life is the making-one of Mind and Soul; accordingly Death is not the destruction of those that are at-oned, but the dissolving of their union.

15. Æon, moreover, is God's image; Cosmos [is] Æon's; the Sun, of Cosmos; and Man, [the image] of the Sun.

The people call change death, because the body is dissolved, and life, when it's dissolved, withdraws to the unmanifest. But in this sermon *(logos)*, Hermes, my beloved, as thou dost hear, I say the Cosmos also suffers change,—for that a part of it each day is made to be in the unmanifest,—yet it is ne'er dissolved.

These are the passions of the Cosmos—revolvings and concealments; revolving is conversion and concealment renovation.

16. The Cosmos is all-formed,—not having forms external to itself but changing them itself within itself. Since, then, Cosmos is made to be all-formed, what may its maker be? For that, on the one hand, He should not be void of all form; and, on the other hand, if He's all-formed, He will be like the Cosmos. Whereas, again, has He a single form, He will thereby be less than Cosmos.

What, then, say we He is?—that we may not bring round our sermon *(logos)* into doubt; for naught that mind conceives of God is doubtful.

He, then, hath one *idea,* which is His own alone, which doth not fall beneath the sight, being bodiless, and [yet] by means of bodies manifesteth all [ideas]. And marvel not that there's a bodiless idea.

17. For it is like the form of reason *(logos)* and mountain-tops in pictures. For they appear to stand out strongly from

the rest, but really are quite smooth and flat.

And now consider what is said more boldly, but more truly!

Just as man cannot live apart from Life, so neither can God live without [His] doing good. For this is as it were the life and motion as it were of God—to move all things and make them live.

18. Now some of the things said should bear a sense peculiar to themselves. So understand, for instance, what I'm going to say.

All are in God [but] not as lying in a place. For place is both a body and immovable, and things that lie do not have motion.

Now things lie one way in the bodiless, another way in being made manifest.

Think, [then], of Him who doth contain them all; and think, that than the bodiless naught is more comprehensive, or swifter, or more potent, but *it* is the most comprehensive, the swiftest, and most potent of them all.

19. And, thus, think from thyself, and bid thy soul go unto any land; and there more quickly than thy bidding will it be. And bid it journey oceanwards; and there, again, immediately 'twill be, not as if passing on from place to place, but as if being there.

And bid it also mount to heaven; and it will need no wings, nor will aught hinder it, nor fire of sun, nor aether, nor vortex-swirl, nor bodies of the other stars; but, cutting through them all, it will soar up to the last Body [of them all]. And shouldst thou will to break through this as well, and contemplate what is beyond—if there be aught beyond the Cosmos; it is permitted thee.

20. Behold what power, what swiftness,

thou dost have! And canst thou do all of these things, and God not [do them]?

Then, in this way know God; as having all things in Himself as thoughts, the whole Cosmos itself.

If, then, thou dost not make thyself like unto God, thou canst not know Him. For like is knowable to like [alone].

Make, [then], thyself to grow to the same stature as the Greatness which transcends all measure; leap forth from every body; transcend all Time; become Eternity; and [thus] shalt thou know God.

Conceiving nothing is impossible unto thyself, think thyself deathless and able to know all,—all arts, all sciences, the way of every life.

Become more lofty than all height, and lower than all depth. Collect into thyself all senses of [all] creatures,—of fire [and] water, dry and moist. Think that thou art at the same time in every place,—in earth, in sea, in sky; not yet begotten, in the womb, young, old, [and] dead, in after-death conditions.

And if thou knowest all these things at once,—times, places, doings, qualities, and quantities; thou canst know God.

21. But if thou lockest up thy soul within thy body, and dost debase it, saying: I nothing know; I nothing can; I fear the sea; I cannot scale the sky; I know not who I was, who I shall be—what is there [then] between [thy] God and thee?

For thou canst know naught of things beautiful and good so long as thou dost love thy body and art bad.

The greatest bad there is, is not to know God's Good; but to be able to know [Good], and will, and hope, is a Straight Way, the Good's own [Path], both leading there and easy.

If thou but sett'st thy foot thereon, 'twill meet thee everywhere, 'twill everywhere be seen, both where and when thou dost expect it not,—waking, sleeping, sailing, journeying, by night, by day, speaking, [and] saying naught. For there is naught that is not image of the Good.

22. *Her.* Is God unseen?

Mind. Hush! Who is more manifest than He? For this one reason hath He made all things, that through them all thou mayest see Him.

This is the Good of God, this [is] His Virtue,—that He may be made manifest through all.

For naught's *unseen*, even of things that are without a body. Mind sees itself in thinking, God in making.

So far these things have been made manifest to thee, Thrice-greatest one! Reflect on all the rest in the same way within thyself, and thou shalt not be led astray.

LESSON I.

The All and Good

1. *Mind.* Master this sermon *(logos),* then, Thrice-greatest Hermes, and bear in mind the spoken words; and as it hath come unto Me to speak, I will no more delay.

Hermes. As many men say many things, and these diverse, about the All and Good, I have not learned the truth. Make it, then, clear to me, O Master mine. For I can trust the explanation of these things, which comes from Thee alone.

Mind. Master this sermon *(logos),* then, Thrice-greatest Hermes, and bear in mind the spoken words; and as it hath come unto Me to speak, I will no more delay.

The present sermon is directed to Hermes by the Mind. This being the case, we are to understand it as being in the nature of an Initiation of Hermes into the Hidden Wisdom, the Initiator being the Mind. Hermes, when viewed Cosmically is the Cosmic Reason or Logos, and when viewed as a man, he is the physical incarnation or Avatar of that Reason. It makes no difference whether we think of Hermes here as being the God Thoth, or as being the man, Hermes Trismegistus, in either case he will be the Cosmic Reason, in the first instance, the Cosmic Reason in its free state, but in the second instance, the Cosmic Reason functioning as the reason in the Avatar Hermes Trismegistus. In either case we have the Reason being instructed by the Mind. The expression, "as it hath come unto Me to speak," shows that the Mind here is not God-the-Mind, but rather the Mind as God's very essence, the Mind as energy of God, Mind as Soul of God that is here speaking, seeing that it had come unto Mind to speak, for it would come unto this Mind from God-the-Mind, but nothing could possibly come unto God seeing that all originates within Him. It is in fact the God-Mind fecundating Ku with Thoughts which are manifested as the Thought Energy in the Mind as Soul of God. This Mind thinks these Thoughts, which acting upon the Logos or Reason are uttered as Ideas, which in this way are manifested in Hermes as Reason. Our *logos* then is what the Mind conceives within the Reason and within the reason of Hermes. He is instructed to master this logos in the sense of becoming this *logos*, in a word, he must incarnate this wisdom which he is to receive. He must also hold these words in his mind, so that they will be born as thoughts in his mind, thus, it is both in the mind and in the reason that these truths must manifest themselves, the *logos* must be incarnate both in the mind and in the reason of Hermes, and in this way will his mind and his reason be regenerated by the words of the Mind. Therefore, we have here the spontaneous action of the Mind upon the reason and the mind of Hermes.

Hermes. As many men say many things, and these diverse, about the All and Good, I have not learned the truth. Make it, then, clear to me, O Master mine! For I can trust the explanation of these things, which comes from Thee alone.

The subject matter of this entire sermon is the All and Good. In a word, we are to learn about God as the All, and God as the Good. This expression, the All, is one that we must not misunderstand. It does not mean the sum-total of all things taken collectively, but rather the unmanifest All, in Whom all things subsists as to their germs of life, that which contains within It the *norms* of all things. It is God in the sense of the Fecund Womb of Life, fecundated with the Germs of all particular lives.

The Good is also God in the feminine sense, in other words, both refer to the Femininity of God, to the Divine Motherhood or Divine Maternity. The remark of Hermes indicates that it is the man Hermes Trismegistus that we have to deal with here. Many men say many things about the All and Good, but no two of them say the same thing, but Hermes is not fooled by any theory of points of view, and diverse angles of truth, he knows full well, that there can be but one true view as to the essence of the All and Good, and therefore, these people are wrong. It is for this reason that he has not learned the truth, and he is sure that no man knows any thing about the subject, hence he cannot trust the explanation of any of the teachers relative to this subject. He knows that whatever comes to him from the Mind, will be the Absolute Truth, because the Mind is merely the radiating energy of God, and hence, all that the Mind gives will be the consciousness of God in action. From this, we see that what our sermon contains is the last word on the subject of the All and God, it is the very Wisdom of God, being what God knows about the subject, and hence there is no room for opinion in the matter, every word in this sermon is infallibly correct. These words are all God-words, and from their mandate there is no appeal in Time or in Eternity. For this reason, it is essential that we harken to all that is said here, for God Himself knows no more about it than is contained here in our sermon. Let it be understood that this applies with equal force to every statement in the sermon, there is not a single error, or a single statement that can ever be improved upon in all that Mind gives to Hermes.

2. *Mind.* Hear [then], My son, how standeth God and All.

God; Æon; Cosmos; Time; Becoming.

God maketh Æon; Æon, Cosmos; Cosmos, Time; and Time, Becoming.

The Good,—the Beautiful, Wisdom, Blessedness,—is essence; as it were of God; of Æon, Sameness; of Cosmos, Order; of Time, Change; and of Becoming, Life and Death.

The energies of God are Mind and Soul; of Æon, lastingness and deathlessness; of Cosmos, restoration and the opposite thereof; of Time, increase and decrease; and of Becoming, quality.

Æon is, then, in God; Cosmos, in Æon; in Cosmos, Time; in Time, Becoming.

Æon stands firm round God; Cosmos is moved in Æon; Time hath its limits in the Cosmos; Becoming doth become in Time.

Mind. Hear [then], My son, how standeth God and All.

The subject matter of the sermon is here indicated to be God and the All as the Unity of His manifestations. It is the relation in which the All stands to God as its Source. The All is here contrasted with God, being taken as all else than God, in the sense of being the several stages of the manifestation and emanation which comes forth from God.

God; Æon; Cosmos; Time; Becoming.

These are the Five Stages of Being, under one of which, every phase of life must be directly brought into being. Apart from these Five Aspects of Being, there is nothing, there never has been anything, and there never will be anything. First we have God, Who manifests in Æon, which in turn is manifested in Cosmos, which manifests in Time, and this latter expresses itself in Becoming. All the acts of God are transformed by Æon, Cosmos, Time and Becoming in order that they may become forms of concrete life. All the acts of Æon must be transformed by Cosmos, by Time, and by Becoming, in order to become Concrete. All Cosmic operations must be transformed in terms of Time and of Becoming, in order that they may become Concrete and all the operations of Time must be transformed in terms of Becoming, ere they may become Concrete. In this way we see that there are four intermediaries between God and the Objective World, two between Cosmos and the Objective World, and one between Time and the Objective World while the Objective World is generated in Becoming.

God Maketh Æon; Æon, Cosmos; Cosmos, Time; and Time, Becoming.

Here we learn that Æon is the product of God. This means that as a result of the functioning of God, Æon is spontaneously generated by such functioning of God, not that God deliberately wishes to make Æon, but rather that the Life of God becomes Æon. In the same way, the activity of Æon spontaneously generates Cosmos, not that Æon wishes to make Cosmos, but rather that the Life of Æon becomes Cosmos. Likewise, the activity of Cosmos spontaneously generates Time, not that Cosmos has any desire to make Time, but rather that the activity and Life of Cosmos, becomes Time. In like manner, the activity of Time generates Becoming, in the sense that of itself, this activity and Life of Time becomes Becoming. We are not here dealing with Design, but rather with the spontaneous fruitfulness of all these manifestations of Life. These Five Categories are connected as Cause and Effect, God being the Ultimate Cause of all, and Becoming the Subsequent Effect of all, and the other three, being both Effect of that which is above, and Cause of that which is below them. God is the Cause of Æon. Æon is the Effect of God, and the Cause of Cosmos. Cosmos is the Effect of Æon and the Cause of Time. Time is the Effect of Cosmos and the Cause of Becoming. Becoming is the Effect of Time and the Cause of all things that become.

The Good,—the Beautiful, Wisdom, Bles-

sedness,—is essence, as it were, of God! of Æon, Sameness; of Cosmos, Order; of Time, Change; and of Becoming, Life and Death.

The expression, as it were, of God indicates that it is not exactly correct to speak of the essence of God, seeing that God is super-essential, seeing that He is beyond be-ing. With this reservation as to the use of the term, the essence of God is the Good, the Beautiful, Wisdom and Blessedness. God is full of Beauty, Wisdom and Blessedness, and He alone is Good. It has been shown in Philosophia Hermetica and in Scientifica Hermetica what is meant by the Good, and why we cannot apply the term to any one else than God, so there is no need to go into that here. The same is true of Beauty. He is the Pleroma of Good and Beauty. At the same time is He the Pleroma of Wisdom. Wisdom is at all times to be contrasted with Knowledge. Knowledge has to deal with Particulars, and hence, Wisdom has to deal with Universals. Wisdom, or the understanding of Universals is an essence of God, seeing that it is the act of the Divine Intelligence that causes all Universals to *be*. Wisdom in this sense is that permanent state of Mind which keeps Universals in their state of Sameness, in a word, Universals are Universals because they perpetually subsist in the Divine Mind, and Wisdom is, therefore, the stability of those Universals in the Mind of God as permanent mental states. The Wisdom of God is, therefore, identical with the fundamental Modes of Thought of the Divine Mind. Blessedness is the state of being blessed. To Bless one is to render one Good or Excellent. It means also to confer one's goodness or excellence on another. Blessedness is that quality of goodness and excellence which one confers in the act of blessing another. This quality or essence of Blessedness subsists in God, and is radiated forth when He blesses any one, for to bless one is merely to magnetize one as it were with this quality or essence of Blessedness, the action of which is to produce the state of Bliss. Bliss is the state resulting from one being energized by Blessedness.

Blessedness, then, is the Essence, to Bless one, is the act by which this Essence of Blessedness energizes another, while Bliss is the state or condition resulting from the energizing of any one of the essence of Blessedness. He means to say that all Blessedness subsists in God as an essence of God. That which constitutes God God is that He is the Pleroma of Good, Beauty, Wisdom and Blessedness. In other words, an essence is the be-ing of that of which it is the essence, therefore, God's be-ing is the Good, the Beautiful, Wisdom and Blessedness. The be-ing of God if we might use the term, is identical with the activity and functioning of God. God acts or functions as the Good, the Beautiful, Wisdom and Blessedness. It is this fourfold activity and functioning as the Good, the Beautiful, Wisdom and Blessedness that constitutes Him God. These are the Four Spōntaneities of God.

The essence of Æon is Sameness. Æon's be-ing is Sameness, or the quality of being *Same* as God. From this we are to learn that Æon is not *other* than God, but is the *same* as God. Æon is, therefore, of the essence of God. Not only is this true, however, but the essence of Æon is Sameness in the sense that the be-ing of Æon is in that He is ever the same that He has ever been. Stability and permanence are the qualities of Æon. There is never any change in Æon. This is due to the fact that God never changes, and as Æon is but the continuation of the essence of God, there can be no change in Æon, seeing that Æon is forever the Same as God. The essence of Cosmos is Order, in the sense that Cosmos is that which is Ordered forth by the action of Æon. The Goodness, Beauty, Wisdom and Blessedness of God establish their Sameness in Æon, the energizing of this Sameness, ordering the Cosmos with Its Order, which is the essence of the Cosmos, in the sense that is the be-ing of Cosmos, that quality that constitutes Cosmos and perpetuates it. We are speaking here of course of the Intelligible Cosmos, which is the Order of the Sameness of Æon. The Essence of Time is Change, in the Sense of Transformation. It is in Time that

Same in reality becomes *Other*, hence it is the essence of Cosmos to change *Same* into *Other*, the *othering* of *same* is, therefore, the essence and the quality of Time. It is Time, therefore, that transforms Universals into Particulars, hence Time is the Particularizer. Particularity is, therefore, of the essence of Time. It is in this way that Change is the essence of Time, and the periodicity of these changes is what constitutes Time what He is. The essence of Becoming is Life and Death, or Genesis and Decomposition or dissolution. Life and Death are the two phases of Becoming, Dead things become alive, and Live things become dead, and so is established the periodicity between the two stated, which is the very be-ing of Becoming.

The Energies of God are Mind and Soul; of Æon lastingness and deathlessness; of Cosmos, restoration and the opposite thereof; of Time, increase and decrease; and of Becoming, quality.

We have seen what the essences of God, Æon, Cosmos, Time and Becoming are, we must now see what are their respective energies. By their essences we are to understand those activities that constitute them what they are, that constitute their be-ing, but by their energies we are to understand the modes of their activities on other things, their radiating energies so to speak. The energies of God are Mind and Soul. There are two energies radiated forth from God, one of these becomes Mind, while the other becomes Soul. Nous and Psyche as Substances are the energies of God, and are directly radiated forth from God. Mind is the masculine energy of God the Father, and Soul is the feminine energy of God the Mother or Ku. The energies of Æon are lastingness and deathlessness. By this we are to understand that Æon sends forth an energy the action of which is to confer on whatever it energizes the attribute of lastingness, that is to say, that which will make it last or endure. Likewise, Æon sends forth an energy the action of which is to render whatever it energizes deathless, or to keep them from dying. These energies therefore, counteract the tendency to disintegrate, and likewise do they establish the tendency to endure for all time. The energies of Cosmos are restoration and the opposite of it. One of the energies of Cosmos has the effect of restoring all things to their former condition, and the other energy has the effect of preventing this restoration, or in other words of transforming them from their former state to some other state. The Cosmic life is the result of the perpetual conflict between these two energies, the one differentiating all things, and the other restoring all things back as they were before. The order of Cosmos is the result of the struggle between these two energies. It is in this way that the Cosmic Order is one ever changing, and yet, ever the same. The energies of time are increase and decrease. Time has two energies, the effect of the one is to increase and nourish all things, so that their growth is promoted, while the other exhausts them through decrease, so that they are prepared for the change that will in turn lead to genesis of another state. It is thus that the essence of Change, manifests actively as the two energies of increase and decrease, for all changes are wrought through increase and decrease. The energy of Becoming is quality. It is through the action of Becoming, the essence of which is Life and Death, that the energy of quality is generated and acts upon all things in such a way as to energize them with their qualities. All things derive their qualities from the energizing of the quality of Becoming.

Æon is, then, in God; Cosmos, in Æon; in Cosmos, Time; in Time, Becoming.

Æon ever abides in God, having its root and source in God. Cosmos ever abides in Æon, having its root and source firmly planted in Æon. Time ever abides in Cosmos, having its root and source firmly planted in Cosmos. Becoming ever abides in Time, having its root and source firmly planted in Time. For this reason, Æon is energized by the energy of God, from which it derives its essence, Cosmos is energized by the energy of Æon, from which it derives its essence, Time is energized by Cosmos, from which it derives its essence, and Becoming is energized by Time from which it derives its essence. Æon subsists in God while God exists in Æon. Cosmos subsists in Æon while Æon exists in Cosmos. Time subsists in Cosmos, while Cosmos exists in Time. Becoming subsists in Time, while Time exists in Becoming, and also, Becoming exists in all things, while all things subsists in Becoming.

Æon stands firm round God; Cosmos is moved in Æon; Time hath its limits in the Cosmos; Becoming doth become in Time.

The terms made use of here indicate the **exact** differences between the diverse Principles. Æon stands firm round God. This means that God is the Center manifesting as Æon, however, we are not to understand that Æon is the boundary enclosing God, for God is more extended if we can speak of extension with reference to God, than all else beside, but Æon stands round God in the sense of God being the Source of the Essence of Æon. Æon stands firm round God, in the sense of being stability, being immovable, and transcending all space as well as all time. The center of all then is both God and Æon, they collectively constituting one center, so that Æon is never separated from God, nor can Æon ever be rendered distinct from God, being God's Eternity of Energy. Cosmos is moved in Æon. Cosmos is in motion, and all the motions of Cosmos transpire within Æon, for Æon is the Space of Cosmos. Not that we are to think of the Intelligible Cosmos as a Body moving from one point of Æon to another, for Cosmos as a whole never shifts its position, but all of the diverse parts of Cosmos are in motion, and Cosmos is the sum-total of all those moving parts, and they all move in Æon. Time has its limits in Cosmos. This means that Time is accomplished in Cosmos. The Change which is the Essence of Time, manifesting through increase and decrease which are the energies of Time, is accomplished within

Cosmos, and never outside of Cosmos. Time is in reality that periodicity of change that extends down from the Intelligible Cosmos, being engendered by the Intelligible Cosmos, it is in fact the process through which Universals produce Particulars, hence Time functions within the Order of Cosmos, as an extension of that Order and not as something distinct from it. Becoming becomes in Time, that is all becomings are conditioned by Time, and are in fact products of Time. Thus, there are really four stages or Zones of the Cosmos, the Intelligible Cosmos, Time or the Temporal Cosmos, Becoming, or the Generating Cosmos, and lastly that which is generated through Becoming or genesis, the Sensible Cosmos. All becomings are, therefore, subject to Time, in the sense of Periodicity. As Becoming becomes in Time, it follows that all becomings are subject to, and conditioned by Time, hence, all becomings are temporal. Seeing that Time is Periodicity, therefore, all things become periodically, that is, there is a beginning and an end to all things that become. The essence of Becoming being Life and Death, whatever becomes must live and die. Becoming in Time, all things that become are subject unto increase and unto decrease. This being the case, it is utterly out of the question for God to create something that will not die. Whatever is created, must be created in Time, for there was of necessity a period when it was not yet created, hence a period before it had become, and there will then of necessity be a period after it has ceased to be, hence God cannot create that which will endure for all Eternity, seeing that all creations are in time. It is for this reason that the Buddha in his transcendent wisdom taught that whatever has been engendered must also be dissolved, for it is engendered in Time, and it must be dissolved in Time, seeing that it has become, it must likewise disappear. All becomings become in Time, and hence, the temporality of all becomings is their most fundamental quality, and as their quality is absolutely derived from Becoming, seeing that this quality has become through the action of their becoming, they can have no other quality than the temporal. Eternity is never the quality of any thing that has become, hence nothing is Eternal, but all things are Temporal. The full force of this will appear more plainly to us as we go on with our examination of this logos.

LESSON II

God and Æon

3. The source, therefore, of all is God; their essence, Æon; their matter, Cosmos.

God's power is Æon; Æon's work is Cosmos—which never *hath* become, yet ever *doth* become by Æon.

Therefore will Cosmos never be destroyed, for Æon's indestructible; nor doth a whit of things in Cosmos perish, for Cosmos is enwrapped by Æon round on every side.

Her. But God's Wisdom,—what is that?

Mind. The Good and Beautiful, and Blessedness, and Virtue's all, and Æon.

Æon, then, ordereth [Cosmos], imparting deathlessness and lastingness to matter.

The source, therefore, of all is God; their essence, Æon; their matter, Cosmos.

God is the source of all things, in the sense that the activity or functioning of God is the initial cause of all things coming into being. This is due to the fact that the primal source of any thing is a corresponding Thought in the Divine Mind, and the enforming of that Thought in Ku or the Divine Maternity as the Good and the Beautiful. It is in this way that the source of each and every thing is to be found in God. In like manner, the essence of of all things is in Æon. It is the essence of a thing that constitutes its be-ing, and it is the activity of Æon that causes all things to *be*. By this we are to understand that the enformed Thought of God, which is the source of a thing, in the sense of being the Idea of that thing, entering into Æon, receives its essence, by which it comes into be-ing. At this stage it is merely Idea and Essence, but has taken on no such thing as form. The matter of all things is Cosmos. By this we are to understand that a thing does not pass from its condition as essence, to its condition as form, until it has entered Cosmos, and there receives the matter essential to the conferring of form upon it. God then is the source, of a thing, Æon gives it its essence, and Cosmos confers upon it the form through the action of this essence on the matter of Cosmos.

God's power is Æon; Æon's works is Cosmos—which never *hath* become, yet ever *doth* become by Æon.

The power of God is used in the sense of His Centrifugal Will Force, the positive, dynamic Force of God. It is in this sense that the Power of God is Æon. We are to think of Æon as being the expansiveness of God, the overflow of God as Power so to speak. Cosmos is the work of Æon in the sense that this Æon being Power, must express itself in action, being dynamic, it must express itself in action, and the work wrought by this Power or Æon, is the Cosmos. Thus we may again speak of God as the Source of all Power, of Æon as being the Power engendered by that Source or God, and of Cosmos as being the Work wrought by the Power, or Æon. Cosmos never *hath* become, seeing that Cosmos is the work wrought by Æon, and Æon being essentially Dynamic Power, the essentiality of Æon, is to work, hence, this Power has been working as long as it has been. Æon as Power of God, must have subsisted with God, that is, unless there was a time when God was without power, which is not to be thought of, Æon being the Power of God, must have been in action as long as God has subsisted, hence Æon is as eternal as is God. There can be no Eternal Power, that is devoid of action, and hence, Æon has been working as long as It has been, in other words, the working of Æon is as eternal as is Æon, which means as eternal as is God. The work of Æon being Cosmos, it follows that Æon has been producing Cosmos as long as Æon has *been* hence, throughout all Eternity, Cosmos has *been*. This being the case, Cosmos hath never *become* in the sense of first coming into being, for there was never a point in Duration when Cosmos will not be. However, Cosmos is forever becoming through the action of Æon. Therefore, we must not think of Cosmos as being a *thing*, produced at some point in time, but rather as being the perpetual working of Æon, and as being the work of Æon taking form, which, at a given point in Duration, is the work of Æon at that point. Thus Cosmos is ever in a state of Flux, being the enforming of the work of Æon which is the Dynamic Power of God. Cosmos then is the process of Æon's working, rather than a thing produced by Æon. You will never be able to understand the nature of Cosmos as long as you think of it as a *thing*, you must learn to think of Cosmos as an inworking process, or sequence of inworkings of the Dynamic Power of Æon in the Primal Substance which we term Matter in this connection. Cosmos then, is both the Primal Matter, and likewise it is the sequential in-working of the active power of Æon in that Primal Matter. Thus Cosmos is the beginningless and endless sequence of becoming, and yet there never was a time when it was not, just as it is now. It is for this reason that Cosmos is ever changing, and yet ever the same, ever becoming, and yet there never was a time when it was not, just as it is now. It is for this reason that Cosmos is ever changing, and yet ever the same, ever becoming, and yet it forever is. Therefore, think of Cosmos as the Eternal Work of Æon, rather than as an object produced by Æon's workmanship.

Therefore will Cosmos never be destroyed, for Æon's indestructible; nor doth a whit of things in Cosmos perish, for Cosmos is enwrapped by Æon round on every side.

Cosmos can never be destroyed for the reason that Cosmos is not an organism that may be disintegrated. All bodies that have been organized are destined to be disorganized. All compounds must be dissolved, and all constructed things are doomed to destruction. Cosmos, however, is not any thing of this nature. It has not been composed, therefore, it can never be decomposed. Seeing that Cosmos is a work wrought by active power, it will of necessity continue so long as the working of that active power continues. Cosmos being a state of working, rather than a thing, the only way for it to be destroyed would be for the working of that power to cease. Being the Power of God, Æon is indestructible, for the duration of God's Power is as the duration of God, and hence this Power which is Æon can never cease. Æon being power must act, for power is but the potentiality for action, and all action must produce results, that is, it must work, therefore, the duration of Æon's working is as the duration of Æon, hence, the working of Æon can never cease, and as Cosmos is the work of Æon, in the sense of the continuity of Æon's working, it can only be destroyed by the destruction of Æon, which can only be consummated by the destruction of God, which can not be. Therefore, will Cosmos never be destroyed, for God cannot be apart from Power, and God's power is Æon, therefore, God cannot *be* apart from Æon, and Æon lives only in Its work, and as that work is Cosmos, neither God nor Æon can *be* without at the same time manifesting the work which is Cosmos. Cosmos being enwrapped round about by Æon, no power but that of Æon can ever enter Cosmos, and hence nothing transpires in Cosmos, unless it be the work of Æon, hence all Cosmic motions are moved by Æon, therefore, there is nothing in Cosmos that is not the working of Æon. All the things that are in Cosmos being the work of Æon, they are all of necessity, Eternal. No single thing in Cosmos will, therefore, ever be destroyed. No whit of things in Cosmos can ever perish, they are each and all as lasting as is God Himself. Needless to say, we are speaking here of the Intelligible Cosmos, not of the Sensible Cosmos. Cosmos is God in Manifestation, and all of the motions of Cosmos are Divine as God Himself is Divine. As Cosmos is moved in Æon, it follows that It is moved in Eternity, hence all the motions in Cosmos are Eternal and none of them are Temporal. This Cosmos, therefore, transcends Time in all of its movements, seeing that all of the movements in Cosmos are works of Æon, which is the Eternity of the Power of God, in action.

Her. But God's Wisdom—what is that?

We have seen how Æon is the Power of God, and the way in which this Power is working, and how its work is Cosmos. In view of this we naturally ask, what is the Wisdom of God? In what way is it related to Cosmos? To understand the trend of this line of reasoning, one must bear in mind that God functions Power, which power is Æon, that Æon as Divine Essence works, and Its work is Cosmos. This being the case, all of the Attributes of God must of necessity function through Æon and Cosmos, and what we want is to trace each of these Attributes of God, through Æon and Cosmos, and see in what way God is manifested in His entirety in the Universe. The question here is, what is God's Wisdom? How does it work in Cosmos? And what effect does it have upon the workings and movements of Cosmos?

Mind. The Good and Beautiful, and Blessedness, and Virtue's all, and Æon.

We are assured that the Wisdom of God is made up of the Good, the Beautiful, all that belongs to Virtue, and also the Æon. All of these collectively, constitute the Wisdom of God. The Wisdom of God is to be understood as that Mental state of visualization by which the Thoughts of God take shape as the Cosmos. Cosmos is a picture of the universe, and we are to think of it rather as first, a mental image in the Mind of God, which being reflected becomes the Intelligible Cosmos, which in turn, acting through Matter, takes form as the universe. God's Wisdom is, therefore, His Creative

Thought, which Orders into being the Cosmos. Into this Wisdom enters all of the Good, the Beautiful, Blessedness, Virtue and Æon. We have already seen that Æon is the Eternal Power of God. Virtue is Virile Force, hence, the Virility of God the Father, and the statement that all pertaining to Virtue goes to constitute Wisdom, means that into this Creative Thought of God there enters all of His Paternal Virility, hence, His Spermal Seed. This Wisdom contains Blessedness, for the reason that it is through this imaging of His Thought that God confers Bliss upon all, He blesses through the action of His Creative Thought. The Good and the Beautiful being Feminine Principles, they refer to the entrance of the Muliebrity of God the Mother into this Wisdom of God, so that God through this action of Visualizing the Creative thought into Cosmos, bring to bear, all the masculine and all the feminine potencies of the Divine Esse and Essence, which are all manifested in Cosmos, and for this reason is Cosmos the Second God and Image of the First God.

Æon, then, ordereth [Cosmos], imparting deathlessness and lastingness, to matter.

Seeing that all of the Attributes of God are present in Æon as essence, the action of Æon will be as the action of all of the Attributes of God. This Æon which is Essence of God in which are present all of God's Attributes, works in Cosmos, and Cosmos is nothing more than the working Æon. Thus Cosmos ordered by Æon, in the sense of Æon working as Positive and Active Force, which acting upon Primal Matter moves it in such way as to order its motions, so that all of the workings of Æon are present in Cosmos as works, thus is Cosmos the ordered work of Æon. Deathlessness and Lastingness being characteristic of Æon, they are of course ordered into Cosmos, so that they are fundamental characteristics of Cosmos likewise. For this reason, Cosmos is in itself deathless and lasting, and hence there can be nothing else in any part of Cosmos. Not only is this true, but through the action of

Æon upon Cosmos, and of Cosmos upon Matter, we find that deathlessness and lastingness are characteristics of matter itself. Æon is Eternity, Cosmos is Eternal and Matter is Deathless, though not Eternal, that is, it is rendered deathless through its being energized by Æon, though it would not be deathless without such energizing.

4. For its becoming doth depend on Æon, as Æon doth on God.

Now Genesis and Time, in Heaven and on Earth, are of two natures.

In Heaven they are unchangeable and indestructible, but on the Earth they're subject unto change and to destruction.

Further, the Æon's soul is God; the Cosmos's soul is Æon; the Earth's soul, Heaven.

And God's in Mind; and Mind, in Soul; and Soul, in Matter; and all of them through Æon.

But all this Body, in which are all the bodies, is full of Soul; and Soul is full of Mind and [Mind] of God.

It fills it from within, and from without encircles it, making the All to live.

Without, this vast and perfect Life [encircles] Cosmos; within, it fills [it with] all lives; above, in Heaven, continuing in sameness; below, on Earth, changing becoming.

For its becoming doth depend on Æon, as Æon doth on God.

The Becoming, or Genesis of Matter depends upon the working in Matter of Æon, in just the same way that the be-ing of Æon depends upon the active functioning of God. It is the working of Æon in Matter that gives to Matter the Becoming or Genesis peculiar to Matter. Were it not for this in-working of Æon in Matter, the latter would be without any process of Genesis. Matter then, is the Feminine Principle which being fecundated by the working in it of Æon, conceives through Genesis. Æon is therefore the Masculine Principle of which Matter is the Feminine Consort, and she, Matter, is impregnated by the Seed of Æon, which is the working of Æon in her, and as a result, she becomes fecund, and the result is Genesis. God is both Father and Mother of both Æon and Matter, while Æon is Husband and Matter is Wife, and Matter's Becoming, or Genesis brings forth the Child of both Æon and 'Matter's Becoming, or Genesis brings forth the Child of both Æon and Matter. All therefore, that is generated in Matter is of an Æonian Life, but of a Material Form. Hold this in thy thought, for it will have a very strong bearing upon the subject of the Science of Alchemy as we go on into the deeper principles of our Science.

Now Genesis and Time, in Heaven and on the Earth, are of two natures.

In Heaven they are unchangeable and indestructible, but on the Earth they're subject unto change and to destruction.

All Genesis is in Matter as a result of her having been impregnated by the working of Æon, this work being Cosmos, hence, we are to think of Matter here as not being the same as Cosmos, for Cosmos is the Order of Æon's working, seeing that Cosmos is the Work of Æon, but Matter is that in which and through which, Æon works as Cosmos. Genesis therefore, takes place in Matter, as a result of her having been subjected to the order of Cosmos. This Matter is subject unto two conditions, or rather manifests under two aspects, Genesis and Time. There are two natures of Genesis and Time, one of which pertains to Heaven and the other to the Earth. This is due to the fact that the Matter of Earth is much grosser than is the Matter of Heaven, and hence Time and Genesis in Heaven is of a much finer order than is the Time and Genesis of Earth. Nature means the being born, or the process of coming into birth, and hence there is a heavenly nature, that is, a heavenly process of being born, and likewise an earthly nature, that is an earthly process of being born, in the case of both Time and Genesis. In Heaven both Time and Genesis are unchangeable, in the sense that the nature of Heaven, responding perfectly to the workings of Æon through Cosmos generates in all cases after the image and likeness of the working of Æon, hence the Genesis of Heaven is the perfect expression through Genesis of the Æon, therefore, we may say that the Genesis of Heaven is Æonian. Also, we may say that in the Genesis of Heaven, there is never any such thing as transformation, or differentiation, seeing that the Genesis of Heaven perfectly follows the *Norm* supplied by the Ideal World Order. Likewise, in Heaven, Genesis is continuous and uninterrupted, there being no such thing as periods of Genesis here, but rather an endless sequence of Genesis. This is due to the fact that Genesis in Heaven has to do with essences not with composed bodies. For this reason, Genesis here is continuous, and has no beginning and no ending, For this reason, all Genesis in Heaven is Immortal. On the other hand, Genesis in the Earth is subject to change and to destruction, seeing that on the Earth, Genesis works through composed bodies. Genesis does the work of composing these bodies, and in the course of time, its work is subject unto change, and the bodies are destroyed. This is due to the character of the elements which go into their composition. Also, in Heaven, Time is continuous. Time in Heaven is simply periodicity, and a continued periodicity having no breaks and hence no periods. In the Earth, however, Time is subject unto change and to destruction, seeing that Time itself works through composed bodies, and hence, it is to be seen passing through the same changes and destructions that those composed bodies pass through. Time on Earth is the Time of Composed Bodies, as Genesis is the Genesis of Composed Bodies, while in Heaven, Time is the Time of Essences and Genesis is the Genesis of Essences. Thus it is that the nature of Time and Genesis in Heaven is the nature of Essences, while the Nature of both Time and Genesis in the Earth, is the nature of Composed Bodies.

Further, the Æon's Soul is God; the Cosmos' Soul is Æon; the Earth's Soul, Heaven.

Æon is to be thought of as a body, the soul of which is God. This will mean that Æon is a body of Power and Essence, acted upon directly by God, just as the soul acts upon the body, being passive to God, in such a way that all of the functioning of God manifests in the Essence of Æon as the working of Æon. Æon will in this way be perfectly passible to God. In the same way, Æon is the Soul of Cosmos, which is in turn the Body of Æon. Æon as essence, works in Cosmos as its work, hence the Matter of Cosmos is perfectly passible under the working of Æon. In like manner, Heaven is the Soul of the Earth, and Earth is the Body of Heaven. This will mean that Earth is perfectly passible under the energizing of it by Heaven, and that all of the energies of Heaven are manifested in the Earth as the Body of Heaven. This will apply to Earth in the sense of all Physical Matter and not merely to this Earth on which we live. Thus Heaven and Earth are not distinct and separated the one from the other, but are in reality at-oned as Soul and Body in one being. It is in this way that we are to think of them, Heaven as the Soul of Earth, and Earth as the Body of Heaven.

And God's in Mind; and Mind, in Soul; and Soul, in Matter; and all of them through Æon.

God is in Mind in the sense of Mind being the radiating energy of God, an energy coming from no other source save God alone, and coming directly and immediately from God. Being God in essentiality, Mind is that which conveys God to all else beside. Mind is in Soul in the sense that just as

Mind is the Energy radiating forth from God, it is likewise radiated into Soul, shining into Soul, and energizing Soul by reason of its power. In this same way, Soul is in Matter, in the sense that Matter being purely passible, it is the action of the indwelling Soul that energizes Matter and causes it to move. It is through Æon that all of these relations are brought about. Æon being the Power of God, is what regulates the radiating forth of the Mind as Energy of God. It is likewise the action of Æon as Power of God, and as worker that causes Mind to shine into Soul, and also Æon directs the process of Genesis and Action that causes Soul to energize Matter, hence Æon is the instrument of God in connecting these diverse states of being.

But all this Body, in which are all the bodies, is full of Soul; and Soul is full of Mind, and [Mind] of God.

By this Body we are to understand the Cosmos, but not the Intelligible Cosmos that we have been speaking of, seeing that is above the Plane of Soul, Soul being a product of Cosmos, and related to Time, we have to deal here with the Sensible Cosmos, which is in itself a Body, and hence something composed of elements. It is Cosmos in the sense of the Body in which are present all the diverse bodies or planets and spheres. This Cosmos is, therefore, the sum-total of all the heavenly bodies, conceived nevertheless as an Unity. This Cosmos is full of Soul, for it is Soul acting upon Cosmos that Imparts Motion unto it, and makes it move, a movement on which all of the life of the Cosmos and of its separate parts depends. Cosmos both in whole and in part is energized by Soul. In the same way, Soul is full of Mind, there being no particle of Soul that is not permeated by Mind, which is the Intelligence of Soul, and thus regulates all of the Genesis of Soul in accordance with intelligence. In like manner, Mind is full of God, seeing that Mind is the Energy of God, and energy that has its Esse in God direct. Thus, there is no thinking of Mind that is not the direct expression of God.

It fills it from within, and from without encircles it, making the All to live.

Soul fills the Cosmos from within, completely permeating every part of the vast interior of Cosmos, so that there is not a single part of the Cosmos that is not filled with Soul. At the same time, Soul is more extended than Cosmos, for it completely encircles the entire body of the Cosmos, enclosing Cosmos in Soul. Cosmos is a Body that is moved, and therefore, it must be moved in Space, and Soul is of necessity the Space in which Cosmos as a Body is moved. Not only this, but every body in Cosmos is likewise completely encircled by Soul, as well as being completely filled with Soul. It is from the fact that Cosmos is both filled within, and encircled from without by Soul, that Cosmos is made to live, and it lives as one body, and one life, rather than as a number of distinct bodies and distinct lives, seeing that its life in all of its parts is derived from the action of the one Soul. The same is true of the relation of the Mind to the Soul, and of God to the Mind. God not only fills Mind from within, but also encircles it from without, and Mind not only fills Soul from within, but also encircles it from without.

Without, this vast and perfect Life [encircles] Cosmos; within, it fills [it with] all lives; above, in Heaven, continuing in sameness; below, on Earth, changing becoming.

The vast and perfect Life or Animal spoken of here is Soul, thought of as an Animal or Life. It encircles the Cosmos from without, and acting within the Cosmos, fills it with all lives. This should show us that in all Cosmos there is nothing without soul. The way in which Soul fills the Cosmos with lives, is to individualize itself, in such a manner as to produce from itself innumerable individual souls. These souls are enlivened so as to become lives. It is from these that all the living things in the Cosmos come. Emphatically lives are not generated from Physical Matter, on the contrary, the lives in Cosmos take unto themselves the Physical Matter necessary to provide them with physical bodies. This applies to both the planes of Cosmos, in Heaven as well as in the Earth. These lives in Heaven continue as they are, preserving their nature as souls, but in the Earth, these lives change and thereby become, that is to say, they experience the changes of Life and Death, in the sense that they are born in the bodies, and in turn, die as to their bodies, and later on, reincarnate. All the lives on Earth have lived many physical lives, and have incarnated many times, and are due to reincarnate many times more. Thus we have the lives in Heaven, which never experience any other life than that of souls, and also those that live on Earth is a series of innumerable bodies, but in both cases, these lives come from Soul, and not from Matter.

LESSON III

The Æon Lore

5. And Æon doth preserve this [Cosmos], or by Necessity, or by Foreknowledge, or by Nature, or by whatever else a man supposes or shall suppose. And all is this,—God energizing.

The Energy of God is Power that naught can e'er surpass, a Power with which no one can make comparison of any human thing at all, or any thing divine.

Wherefore, O Hermes, never think that aught of things above or things below is like to God, for thou wilt fall from truth. For naught is like to That which hath no like, and is alone and One.

And do not ever think that any other can possibly possess His power; for what apart from Him is there of life, and deathlessness and change of quality? For what else should He make?

God's not inactive, since all things [then] would lack activity; for all are full of God.

But neither in the Cosmos anywhere, nor in aught else, is there inaction. For that "inaction" is a name that cannot be applied to either what doth make or what is made.

And Æon doth preserve this [Cosmos], or by Necessity, or by Foreknowledge, or by Nature, or by whatever else a man supposes or shall suppose. And all is this, God energizing.

The Cosmos is preserved by Æon. This will of

course be obvious, when we remember that Æon is the Power of God, as well as the Essence, the work of which is the Intelligible Cosmos. This will show that the Intelligible Cosmos is nothing else than the sequential working of Æon, being the Order of that working of Æon in Primal Matter. As the Sensible Cosmos is merely the result of the action of the Intelligible Cosmos on Matter, in such a way as to image itself in Matter, thereby forming a Material Cosmos which exactly corresponds to the Intelligible Cosmos, in other words, ordering Matter in accordance with the Order of Æon's working. It makes no difference whether this Cosmos is preserved by Necessity, or by Foreknowledge, or by Nature, in either case it is Æon that works in this way so as to preserve it. If it be preserved by Necessity, then it is the Chain of Causation that is set in motion and kept in motion by the working of Æon. The activity of Æon it is, that is the initial urge in this sequence of Causation, that determines the working of Cosmos. By Foreknowledge we are to understand that knowledge which knows what is to be, before it comes to pass. Knowledge at all times deals with Things rather than with principles, it is the knowing of things, but Foreknowledge is diverse from the other knowledge in this, that the ordinary Knowledge only knows that which is in existence, but Foreknowledge knows that which will come into existence at a time subsequent to the time the Foreknowledge is exercised. Now, we know that all things come into being by reason of the action of the Intelligible Cosmos on Matter, and as this action in the Intelligible Cosmos is nothing else than the working of the Æon as Power, it follows that it is the working of Æon that brings all things to be, hence, Foreknowledge must of necessity be a foreknowledge of the manner in which Æon will work. As Æon is both Power of God and Essence of God, it must need be that all that is in God will be manifested in Æon as essence. This being obviously true, it follows that the Divine Mind must manifest in Æon, hence Æon must *think*. From this it will follow that the working of Æon will be the result of Æon as Mind, determining the working of Æon as

Power, hence the Foreknowledge of Æon, is that Attribute of Æon by which all works are first thought of, and imaged in mind, before they are expressed in action. Æon must know a thing in Æon, then work it in the Intelligible Cosmos, before it comes to pass in the Sensible Cosmos, hence it is the Foreknowledge of Æon that determines what shall be in Cosmos. And likewise with Nature, she is the process of being born, the activity of Genesis, and it is Æon that works in the Intelligible Cosmos, the Order that orders Matter into action so as to cause Genesis, hence it is Æon that initiates the process of Genesis, and therefore, Nature is nothing else than the working of Æon in that way. In a word, it is the Fecundation of Matter by Æon that confers upon her the power of Genesis, and hence, Nature is the work of Æon. It makes no difference in what way one undertakes to account for the preserving of the Cosmos, in every instance it will be seen to be the work of Æon; for, the Cosmos is preserved by reason of the orderly working of Power in Matter, and the only Power to work in Matter is Æon, hence, Cosmos is preserved by Æon, seeing that Æon is the only Essence that can directly work in Matter, she being passible and having no power of energizing herself. Æon preserves Cosmos, but in doing so, is acting not other than as the Energy of God. It is God energizing that preserves the Cosmos, because Æon is the essence and the power of God, and it becomes the Energy of God, through the energizing of Whom, Cosmos is preserved. The Cosmos is the result of the energizing of Matter, and as it will, therefore, be preserved so long as Matter is energized, and Matter being energized by God through Æon, which is His Eternity, it follows that Matter is Eternally Energized, and therefore, Cosmos is Eternally preserved, hence there can never be an end to Cosmos, for she is made as Eternal as is God himself.

The Energy of God is Power that naught can e'er surpass, a Power with which no one can make comparison of any human thing at all, or any thing divine.

This Energy of God is the active Power of God, and as it is the first or initial energy, it will follow that all other energies and powers are engendered and set in motion by the action of this primal energy and power, hence, they being the products of this Power, will be of less power than will the Power that has engendered them. For this reason, no power will ever be able to surpass this Power of God, but they will all fall short of it, and will be determined by it. In fact there is no other power, energy or thing that can be compared with this Power, neither human or divine thing, is in its class at all. It is from this Energy that all other energies come, hence, no other energy can act except as its action and energizing are conditioned and determined by this Primal Energy and Power. It is through His Energy and Power that God Rules all things, seeing that His Energy is the causative Principle of the causes of all things.

Wherefore, O Hermes, never think that aught of things above or things below is like to God, for thou wilt fall from truth. For naught is like to That which hath no like, and is Alone and One.

There is nothing at all that can be compared to God, for there is nothing like Him. If we look at the process of creation a moment we will be able to see at a glance that it would be out of the question for God to create any thing of like nature to Himself. All things are the result of Matter being energized by the Energy of God; but in all such cases, this energy is transformed by the Matter it is energizing, while God is not influenced by any thing at all, hence, there is nothing like to God. He stands alone, there being nothing that He has not produced, hence, He alone is the unproduced, therefore, there is nothing with which we may compare Him. Seeing that all come from Him, there can never be any one not dependent upon Him for being, and hence there can be nothing that does not partake of that which He gives, hence no one can ever partake of his Esse, which is in the not being dependent upon any thing, or any one for any thing.

And do not ever think that any other can possibly possess His power; for what apart from Him is there of life, and deathlessness and change of quality? For what else should He make?

There is no life apart from God, for things live because of their being energized by God. Apart from Him is there no deathlessness, for all things are rendered deathless by reason of the continuity of their being energized by Him. Apart from Him is there no change of quality, because it is the energizing of all things by God that changes their qualities. In other words, all these conditions are the result of the energizing of all things, and all energy comes from God, there being no other source of energy, apart from Him, nothing would be energized, and hence, apart from Him, there would be no way by which life, deathlessness and change of quality could be brought about. Not only do all others depend upon God for their coming into being, but they likewise depend upon Him to preserve them in their being, hence the continued existence of all depends upon their being continually sustained by the power of God. This being true, nothing can ever possess His Power, which is the power of self-perpetuation, seeing that they depend upon God to perpetuate their existence. There is nothing else for God to make than those which are Himself, that is, He can only manifest forms of Himself, therefore, He does not bring into being, any thing else than Himself. As a result, there is never brought into existence any thing that does not previously subsist in God, hence in all this Cosmos there is no other power save and except the Power of God. As all things are but manifestations of His Power, there can be no other power save that which is in Him.

God's not inactive, since all things [then] would lack activity; for all are full of God.

The Greek word for inactive here is argos, meaning not-working, inactive, idle, a word quite similar to argia, meaning inactivity, idleness. We are informed that God is not argos, and argia cannot be applied to God. On the contrary, the Essence of God is characterized by ergon (work), it is energon (working in, energizing) energes (active, energetic), its quality is energeia (in-working, activity). In other words, the theory of a passive God, one who does nothing, is not true. The very Esse of God is to be active, energetic, to work, to work in, and energize, it is in-working and active in all its attributes. The active, energetic life is then the one that approaches nearest to that of God, and one approaches the nearest to God by an active life, and is the farthest from God by a life of inactivity. The Path of Action then is the one that leads man nearest to God, the Path of Knowledge next, and the Path of Devotion least of all. Quietism is the direct road to Hell rather than the road to Heaven. It is not the Dreamer but the Worker that approaches nearest to God. From this it will be seen that it is the Active Life that leads to Salvation, not the other. God is not inactive, since if this were true, there would be no activity in the Cosmos at all. The contention here is, all things are merely Matter energized by the energies that come from God, hence, there is in reality nothing but God to differentiate things from Matter. Now, as Matter is absolutely passive, it will follow that a thing which is entirely made up of God and Matter, cannot possibly have any activity unless it receives its activity from God, seeing that there is none in Matter. A thing cannot ergon (work) without being energon (active, energetic), and it cannot be thus without the quality of energeia (in-working, activity), and it cannot have this quality without some energon (working in, energizing) force acting upon the Matter composing it. As this is not characteristic of Matter, it must come from some other source, and there is nothing else but God, hence, every one derives his energon (working in, energizing) Principle from God. As he derives it from God, it must of necessity subsist in God in order that one may derive it from God.

This leads to the conclusion that the Essence of God is an energon (working in, energizing) Essence, that it is the very Esse of energeia (in-working, activity). In fact, God is not only active, but activity is not merely one of the Attributes of God, but is His very Esse, just as He is the Esse of activity. He subsists alone in His energia (in-working, activity), were this to cease for an instant, He would die. God is energeia and nothing else. It is from God that all things derive their energeia, it is merely the energia of God energon (working in, energizing) them, and is the ergon (work) of God's energes (active, energetic energeia (in-working, activity). It is for this reason that Sloth has ever been looked upon as one of the Deadly Sins. It is rank rebellion against God.

But neither in the Cosmos anywhere, nor in aught else, is there inaction. For that "inaction" is a name that cannot be applied to either what doth make or what is made.

That which makes a thing, does so through the energetic activity that it brings to bear upon the matter out of which the thing is to be made. Making is in the very nature of things, the process of energizing passive matter. Owing to the passibility of matter, it is moved by energy that acts upon it, hence all things are made through action. The maker makes a thing through the activity of his energy. It is work that makes all things. Things then are made through the activity of the energy making them, hence, nothing that makes another thing is inactive. At the same time, inaction cannot be applied to the things made, for the reason that they are made by reason of the activity of their matter, by the in-working of energy into that matter, thus making it active. Thus it is the working of energy within them that constitutes all things that are made. This being the case, both things that make other things, and likewise things that are made are alike the result of activity, never of inactivity. There can be no inaction in the Cosmos anywhere, for the reason that Cosmos is made up of the making, and of the being made, hence Cosmos is nothing else than the sequence of the in-working, activity, working in and energizing of Matter by Energy, and of the work there consummated. Cosmos then is absolutely active, and nowhere is it inactive.

6. But all things must be made; both ever made, and also in accordance with the influence of every space.

For He who makes, is in them all; not stablished in some one of them, nor making one thing only, but making all.

For being Power, He energizeth in the things He makes and is not independent of them,—although the things He makes are subject to Him.

Now gaze through Me upon the Cosmos that's now subject to thy sight; regard its Beauty carefully—Body in pure perfection, though one than which there's no more ancient one, ever in prime of life, and ever-young, nay, rather, in even fuller and yet fuller prime!

But all things must be made; both ever made, and also in accordance with the influence of every space.

All things must be made, seeing that otherwise they could not be. This is due to the fact that Energy and Matter both go into the makeup of all things, and therefore, Matter must be energized in a particular way in order that the thing may come into being. As a result, things are not Eternal, but must be made, as only Energy is Eternal and Matter is ever-living, but things must be made. They must also be ever made, for the reason that the Arche-Types must perpetually reproduce themselves, therefore, while all things must be made, at the same time, they must forever be, hence their making must be repeated to infinity, seeing that no new thing ever comes into being, and likewise, no thing that has ever been, will ever cease to be, therefore, the making process must continue for ever to reproduce the same types of things. This making must be in accordance with the influence of every space, for the energies that act upon matter in such a way as to energize it, and in that way engender things, must pass through spaces, and the substance of the diverse spaces is different, so, the energy is transformed and differentiated in accordance with the influence upon it, of the spaces through which it passes. In other words, the energizing is conditioned by the influence of the space through which it passes. Likewise, the matter of the things is influenced by the substance of whatever space it is moved through, hence it is the spaces in the universe that determine the character of the making which is wrought in matter by the action of the diverse energies. Another point to be borne in mind in this connection is this: the process of ever making, is a process by which the Arche-types of all things are made, which are the same for all time, they are never changing but at all times preserving the character of their Sameness, at the same time, these Arche-types enter into the diverse spaces in a sense, and there acting upon those spaces, generate counterparts of themselves, conditioned however, by the quality of those particular spaces. Thus, in the Ideal or Intelligible Cosmos there is but the one Arche-type of a thing, which is forever the same as it has always been; but in the diverse spaces, this same Arche-type is differentiated into many Types and differentiations of Types of the original Arche-type. This is in reality what is meant by the Monadic theory of all things. The theory of Things in Themselves is likewise an effort to interpret in terms of consciousness this principle of the Eternal Arche-types of all things. Also, the Atman Theory of India is an effort to express this same proposition of the Arche-types of all things. These things as they are ever made are transformed through Time and Becoming into the things of phenomenal appearance, but the Arche-type as it is ever made, continues forever the same.

> For He who makes, is in them all; not stablished in some one of them, nor making one thing only, but making all.

He who makes here means God. It is God who makes all things, in the sense that the initial energizing comes from Him, and therefore, He is their maker, and the intervening forces are merely the tools made use of by the Divine Maker. He is in all things, in the sense that those energies that are manifestations of His Power, are resident in all the forms that are made. God being the original Energizer, all forms of energy are aspects of Him, and hence, in whatever form energy may be present, there will God likewise be found. It is not that God is established in some one of the things that are made, or that He makes one thing only, but rather is He in all things, and makes all things Himself. This Imminence of God in all things is at first hard to be understood, but if we look at the matter aright, we will see that it is God Himself that is in all things, and that makes all things. God is Esse, and Æon is His Essence and His Power, an Essence that is energes (active, energetic), and energon (working in, energizing). This Æon in its activity is energeia (in-working, activity) in Matter, and its ergon (work), is the Intelligible Cosmos, which energon (working in, energizing) Matter, makes all things, and it is the energizing within the matter of a thing that makes that thing what it is, hence it is the energeia (in-working, activity) of God within a thing that constitutes that thing what it is, that is the Suchness of the thing. It is in this way that God is directly within every thing, and directly makes every thing what it is rather than something else, in a word, God is within each thing the Suchness of that particular thing, it is the Particularization of God that develops the Particular from the Universal. God is then the Esse of each and every thing. He is likewise the Essence of each and every thing.

> For being Power, He energizeth in the things He makes and is not independent of

them—although the things He makes are ject to Him.

In essence, God is Power. Now, it is the essentiality of Power that it shall energize. Being ergon, this Power must work. Being energes, it is active and energetic. Being energeia, it is in-working activity. Being energon, it must work in and energize. Such a Power cannot *be* apart from its in-working activity, its working in and energizing, and these cannot *be* apart from their work. A Power, the essentiality of which is to work, cannot *be* apart from the work it does. This Power is not independent of the things in which it works, for the reason that there can be no energizing, without something energized, hence this working Power, cannot *be* except in its work. The work then is an essential aspect of the Worker, or the Power which is God. Apart from His work, this Power is not, and so God is not, apart from the work He does. God energizeth in the things He makes, seeing that there is nothing else in which He may energize, and seeing that He cannot *be* apart from such energizing; God cannot *be*, apart from the energizing within the things He has made. God cannot *be* without the things he makes, in which His energon is energizing, and therefore, there has never been a time when this Cosmos of Things Made, this Sensible Cosmos, has not been; God is as dependent upon things, as things are dependent upon God. Nevertheless, the things that God makes are subject to Him, seeing that they are because He has made them, and that they continue to be, because He continues to energize them. In a word, the One God, is both Imminent and Transcendent. The Cosmos of Things is full of God, but God is not contained in the Cosmos of Things.

Now gaze through Me upon the Cosmos that's now subject to thy sight; regard its Beauty carefully—Body in pure perfection, though one than which there's no more ancient one, ever in prime of life, and ever-

young, nay rather, in even fuller and yet fuller prime!

When Mind instructs Hermes to gaze through Me, the meaning is that Mind is to be the vehicle of his sight, that he is to gaze with the Eye of the Mind, that is with the Sense pertaining to the Mind. This is a power brought to light in many of the Hermetic Teachings, which it is very hard to grasp, but unless we can understand the meaning of it, we will never understand many of the teachings. It must be borne in mind that there is sense peculiar to the mind in man, a sense that is similar to the senses of the soul, but yet transcending them and in its workings being purely mental. It is through this sense of the mind that the Seeds of Thought enter the mind of man, and there impregnate the mind, so that she conceives thought after their image and likeness. The Mind also has its Sense, through which its Seed of Thought are conveyed to the sense of the mind of a man. The sense of the mind then is a current of Energy, centripetal in the mind of a man, and centrifugal in the Mind. Now, the great problem is to at-one the sense of a man's mind, with the Sense of the Mind, so that they will for the time being, become one sense, and not two distinct senses, so that the mind of the man will have no sense whatsoever apart from the Sense of the Mind, in this way, the sense of the mind of the man, becomes identical with the Sense of the Mind, and therefore, the mind sees with the Sense of the Mind. This condition is what is termed the Eye of Mind, the Eye of Gnosis, and the Eye of Truth. In this state, whatever is sensible to the Mind is likewise sensible to man, while in this state Intelligibles are all rendered perfectly Sensible to him. The instruction of the Mind means that Hermes is to at-one his sense with the Sense of the Mind, so that for the time being he will be endowed with the Eye of Mind, and with this Eye of Mind he is to gaze upon the Cosmos which is subject to his sight, that is, to the sight of the Eye of the Mind. From this we are to understand that it was the Intelligible Cosmos made Sensible to him, that Hermes was to see. This will enable us to understand what is said of this Cosmos. He must not only gaze upon the Cosmos, but he must observe everything about it, and fix his regard upon it, in all of its diverse aspects. Such perception of the Cosmos will impregnate the mind with its Seed, so that this very Cosmos will be conceived in his mind. He is admonished to regard with care, the Beauty of the Cosmos. Remember that Ku is the Beautiful, that is, the One Who is the Pleroma of Beauty. The Beauty of Cosmos therefore, indicates that the Beauty of Ku, is manifested in the Cosmos, that Cosmos is energized by the Beauty of Ku. This Beauty is seen in a Body in pure perfection. The Beauty of Ku is Beauty in Essence, but of course without either form or body. This Essential Beauty of Ku, enters into Matter, and as Essence, energizes Matter with its own energy, in such a way as to energize Matter with its own Beauty, so that in Matter, this Essential Beauty of Ku, becomes the Body of Beauty which is the Beauty of Cosmos. In this way is the Sensible Cosmos rendered the Body of Beauty. At the same time, do not confound this Sensible Cosmos with the Cosmos that is sensible to the Physical Senses in Man, it is rather the Cosmos of Time and Becoming, that is sensible to the senses of the soul and the spirit. It is this Cosmos that presents itself as a Body in pure perfection. There is no more ancient Body than this Body of the Cosmos, because it is the first Body to be engendered, the first thing to be energized, seeing that it is the result of the working of Æon in Matter, the result of the in-working of the Power of God. It is the most ancient of all Bodies, being in fact, the Eternal Body, without beginning and without end. Its duration is simultaneous with the duration of God Himself. At the same time, this Body is ever in prime of life, there never was a time when it was young and there will never be a time when it will grow old, but it is forever the same. At the same time it is ever young, this means that it is forever in a state of perfect maturity, and yet it is forever young, youth and age in one. At the same time, there is here an element of progress in the life of the Cosmos. To understand the nature of the Cosmic Body one must realize a Body, absolutely perfect, and fully developed and mature, and at the same time, one that is forever evolving in a progressive ratio. This is of course difficult to grasp, but until it has been grasped, the true nature of the Cosmic Body is not understood. The key to the mystery is in the fact that Cosmos is in perpetual state of being energized by the Power of God, and that this Power of God is perpetually expressing the Mind of God, a Mind that is perpetually thinking, hence, Cosmos is all the time being energized by the Thought of the Eternally active Mind of God.

LESSON IV

Æonology

7. Behold, again, the seven subject Worlds; ordered by Æon's order and with their varied course full-filling Æon!

[See how] all things [are] full of light, and nowhere [is there] fire; for 'tis the love and blending of the contraries and the dissimilars that doth give birth to light down shining by the energy of God, the Father of all good, the Leader of all order, and Ruler of the seven world-orderings!

[Behold] the Moon, forerunner of them all, the instrument of nature, and the transmuter of its lower matter!

[Look at] the Earth set in the midst of All, foundation of the Cosmos Beautiful, feeder and nurse of things on Earth!

And contemplate the multitude of deathless lives, how great it is, and that of lives subject to death; and midway, between both, immortal [lives] and mortal, [see thou] the circling Moon.

Behold, again, the seven subject Worlds, ordered by Æon's order, and with their varied course full-filling Æon!

The seven subject Worlds, are the seven Worlds subject to Cosmos. They do not mean the Seven Physical Planets of our Solar System; for all of Cosmos is under the sway of these seven subject Worlds, and the vast extent of the Universe was perfectly well known to Hermes, as some of the other sermons amply proclaim. To him, this solar system was a very small part of the Universe. But, these seven subject Worlds contain within them, all of the Cosmos. Remember we are below the Intelligible Cosmos now, we have entered into the realm of Time, or Periodicity, and hence, these seven subject Worlds are in the realm of Time. They are in one sense, the Seven Circles of Heaven (the nature of which has been explained in Scientifica Hermetica, and hence, there is no need for explanation here), and in another sense they are the Seven Secret Planets. These are volumes of Matter filled with specialized Energy and Force, that move through space, traversing the path of the Seven Circles of Heaven, moving round the Spiral Serpent of Time. All the life of the Sensible Cosmos is the result of its being energized by these seven subject Worlds. They are ordered by Æon's order. Æon, it will be remembered is the Power and Essence that works, or energizes in Matter, and its working and energizing, preserves a certain order, which is the manifestation in action, of the essence of Æon. This Order is the Intelligible Cosmos. The statement that the seven subject Worlds are ordered by Æon's order, means that they are ordered by the Intelligible Cosmos. This means that the energizing of Matter by Æon, in that orderly working which is the Intelligible Cosmos, engenders in Matter, Time or Periodicity, which transforms Matter from its Primal to its Heavenly state. This order of Heavenly Matter in Time or Periodicity, orders the Seven Subject Worlds, so that they are energized thereby, and so are ordered, in the sense that they are the manifestations of the working of that energy, they are in fact the seven differentiations of that Order of Cosmos, which thus becomes the Order of each of these seven subject Worlds. With their varied course, the seven subject Worlds fulfill Æon. This means that the completeness and fullness of Æon's energy is all absorbed into the seven subject Worlds, so that it is consumed in their energizing, and hence, all of the working of the energy of Æon is worked in the seven subject Worlds, with their varied course along the path of the Spiral Serpent of Time. Thus do the seven subject Worlds contain within them, and express through their life and action, and their course, the fullness of the energy and energizing of Æon.

[See how] all things [are] full of light, and nowhere [is there] fire; for 'tis the love and blending of the contraries and the dissimilars that doth give birth to light down shining by the energy of God, the Father of all good, the Leader of all order, and Ruler of the seven world-orderings!

He states that everywhere in the realm of the seven subject Worlds there is light, but nowhere is there fire, hence he is contending that those seven subject Worlds are filled with light without fire. The view of many is that light is the reflection from fire, but our Hermes flatly denies the theory that light is a reflection from fire. Also, he repudiates the idea that there is a blending of light and shade in these seven subject Worlds, but teaches on the contrary that light is in a state of universal diffusion throughout the whole of the seven subject Worlds. This universality of light, distinct from fire is what he holds to be the principle characteristic of the seven subject Worlds. If there is no fire, then there is no heat, and hence he is teaching that this universally diffused light is cold light. The question is, from whence comes this light. He holds that light is born as a result of the love and blending of the contraries and the dissimilars. We then have the problem of Opposition introduced here. There is first the differentiation, that causes all things to become diverse, the proposition of *same* becoming *other*, which renders everything contrary to something else, and likewise, dissimilar to something else. We then are no longer in the realm of Universals, but in the realm of Particulars. Particularity, has particularized all things, so that all things are now particular, and hence dissimilar and contrary to each other. At the same time, this process tends to group all things, so that they are thrown into groups, the members of which are similar to each other, though not identical with each other, and therefore, dissimilar to the members of other groups, and even contrary to them. It is this principle of dissimilarity and contrariety that permits synthesis, seeing that without this there would be no distinctions and hence no similarities in things. Strange as it may seem, things are similar to some things, merely because they are dissimilar to other things. It is their contrariety to some things that unites them to other things. It is this working of dissimilarity and contrariety, that enables us to relate some things, and hence relativity is the outgrowth of dissimilarity and contrariety. It is in this way that the Law of Opposites, differentiates all things. But, there is another principle introduced into the workings of this realm, and that is the love and blending of dissimilars and contraries. None of these are complete, for a thing is dissimilar to another, merely because there is in the other, that which is not in it. In a word, dissimilarity is the result of limitation, and hence all things are limited to the extent that they are dissimilar to anything. Their contrariety is due to their one-sideness. Hence, for their completion, these contraries are blended, so as to produce another state, and they love and are united. Through this love of the dissimilars and contraries, opposition is balanced, and so, out of opposition comes balance. The blending of these contraries and dissimilars, leads to a state of rhythm, and hence there grows out of all this Opposition the state of Rhythm. hence the life and evolution in the seven subject Worlds is a process of Motion, Opposition, Balance, and Rhythm. When the opposition of dissimilars and contraries is balanced through their love and blending, the resultant Rhythm is light. This is the true origin of Cosmic light. It shines down by the energy of God. This simply means that all of this process is the result of the energy of God energizing in the seven subject Worlds. This energy which is Æon, energizes in Matter, its energizing being identical with the Intelligible Cosmos, which energizing of Matter, introduces the element of Time or Periodicity, and as a result, Motion is given to all parts of this Cosmos, the Motion engendering Opposition. This Opposition, engenders the state of love and blending in the contraries and the dissimilars, which in the course of time, balances them, and the resultant Rhythm and its light, are therefore, the result of the energizing of the energy of God. God is here spoken of under three designations, the first is the Father of all good. He is this, seeing that He is the Good, in the sense of Principle, and being the Esse of Good, or more properly, Good as Esse, of course it follows that nothing is good save as it is energized by God, hence does all good come from Him. The second designation is that of Leader of all order. Order is merely the working of energy, and as this is the energy of God, it being the initial energy, it follows that all order is merely the working of the order of the energizing of God, hence He Leads all order, seeing that it is His ordering that determines all other order. He is likewise designated as the Ruler of the seven world-orderings. Seeing that the seven worlds are ordered by the previous order of Cosmos, and that, that is but the working of the Æon which is the energy of God, it follows that God, as energy, energizes the Order that orders the seven subject Worlds, so that their ordering is merely the continuation of the ordering of God's energizing, hence He Rules the seven world-orderings. It is from His energizing that light shines down into all things.

[Behold] the Moon, forerunner of them all, the instrument of nature, and the transmuter of its lower matter!

The Moon here, of course, does not mean the visible moon of our Solar System, it rather means the Secret Moon that is one of the seven subject Worlds, and is the Moon to all the Universe and to all of the Cosmic Body. The first statement about this Moon is that she is the forerunner of all of the seven subject Worlds. This means that the Moon leads the procession of the Seven subject Worlds round the

Seven Circles of Heaven. In this way, it is the Moon that first energizes the Matter of space with her energy, before it is ready for the action of the energies of the other six subject Worlds. Next, the Moon is called the instrument of nature. Nature here is equivalent to *nature*, the process of being born, the coming into birth, and hence is equivalent to Genesis. The Moon is the instrument of nature in this sense. It is the Moon through which nature generates all forms. In a word, the Heavenly Matter, in its state of transformation by Time or Periodicity, energized by the energy of the Moon, generates life and form. The Moon is again said to be the transmuter of the lower matter of nature. Here we have nature, as the process of Genesis, and likewise as the matter in which this process of Genesis goes on. This matter is on two Planes, if we may term them so, the higher and the lower. The upper matter is of course perfectly transformed and controlled by nature, but the lower matter, being more gross, and less passible to the energy of nature, offers greater resistance to the transformations and actions of Genesis, and thus it has to be transmuted from the lower to the higher state, from the grosser to the more subtle condition, from the more solid to the more fluidic state, ere it can be acted upon by Genesis. This transmutation of the lower matter of nature, from the gross to the subtle state, is accomplished as a result of its being energized by the energy of the Moon. The energy of the Moon is, therefore, the Alchemical Principle that transmuted the gross matter of nature, into her subtle matter, so that it may become responsive to the action of Genesis, and thereby, may be generated into life and form. This Moon-shine is the real Philosopher's Stone in the Cosmic Alchemy of Nature, and through it nature is able to perpetually give birth to all things, for in this is she *nature*. This is the work of the Secret Moon.

[Look at] the Earth set in the midst of All, foundation of the Cosmos Beautiful, feeder and nurse of things on Earth!

Needless to say, this Earth is not our physical earth. It was perfectly well known to Hermes that this earth was not the center of the Universe. He definitely teaches that it is the Constellation of the Great Bear that moves all of the Cosmos round with it, and therefore, the Great Bear comes nearer being the Center of the Universe than does any thing else; but he teaches that the Great Bear forever turns round its own center of gravity, and hence there is no center to the Universe save that point in empty space that is the center of gravity of the Great Bear. This being the Astronomy of Hermes, it follows of course that he did not mean to teach that this earth on which we live is in the midst of All, least of all did he mean to teach that it is the foundation of the Cosmos. His teaching there is quite clear. If he did not mean our earth, what then did he mean by the Earth? Our logos has traced the creative process from God, through Æon and the Intelligible Cosmos, as the Order of Æon's energizings, into the seven subject Worlds, which it has shown to be orders of energizings, and if they are energizings, there must be something for them to energize. It has shown that Nature was the recipient of the energies of these seven subject worlds, and that she was acting upon matter. The Earth then is identical with this lower matter of Nature, and hence is the Element of Earth used in Alchemical Literature. It is this Earth that is set in the midst of All, seeing that all of the energies of the seven subject Worlds, and of Nature as well as the light, enter into this Elemental Earth, and there work and energize her. As she is the receptacle of all of these energies, and is recipient of them all, she is in the midst of them All. This Earth is the foundation of the Cosmos, because it is the action of nature upon this Element, and its being energized by the energies of the seven subject Worlds, that furnishes the matter out of which all things are organized as bodies. It is in fact the Cosmic protoplasm out of which are made all things. The Cosmos as a Body, is the sum-total of all the things made from Earth by Nature. Therefore, this Earth is the *materia* from which the Cosmic Body is fabricated, and hence it is the foundation of the Sensible Cosmos. It is the feeder and nurse of things on Earth, in the sense of being the substance on which all material things depend for their life and the continuation of their being. Some of these things that are fed and nursed by this Earth, are the suns, moons, planets, including our earth in fact whatever has a gross material body. We are, therefore, dealing with the Element of Earth, as the sustaining power of all material bodies. Of course the physical earth bears the same relation to all the lives upon it, that the Element of Earth does to all material bodies.

And contemplate the multitude of deathless lives, how great it is, and that of lives subject to death; and midway, between both, immortal [lives] and mortal, [see thou] the circling Moon.

We come now to the particular aspect of the Cosmos. We have been looking at its major divisions, but we must now see the diversity of lives that are in it. This Cosmos is filled with vast multitudes of deathless lives, or living things, as well as vast multitudes of lives, or living things that are subject to death. By the deathless lives, we are to understand those lives that have no composed bodies, that is, no bodies compounded of the Four Elements, while all lives subject to death, are such as function in bodies compounded from the Four Elements. All space is filled with these innumerable lives, including Gods, Demi-gods, Daimones, Genii, Heroes, Souls, Spirits, Elementals, Elementaries, Men and the diverse animal and vegetable as well as the Mineral Lives that we have on earth. The line of demarcation between the two spheres, that of the immortal and the mortal lives, is seen in the circular path of the Moon. This means that the realm of matter transmuted by the Moon is the realm of mortal lives, while that realm of matter that is beyond the Moon, and under the control of the other subject Worlds is the habitat of the immortal lives, for it is only out of this perfected matter that the Genesis of immortal lives is possible to nature. The mortal lives are, therefore, generated in the Lunar Sphere, while the immortal lives are generated in the Solar Sphere beyond the sphere of the Moon.

Remember we are speaking here of the seven subject Worlds and the Seven Secret Planets, not of the physical sun and moon. At the same time it may be said that the orbit of the moon of this earth shuts off the deathless lives from the earth, and that the atmosphere and the ether between the earth and the moon, is filled with lives subject to death, but that in that sphere there are no really deathless lives. The latter cannot cross over the line and come this side of the path of the moon. Neither can a life subject to death ever cross over the orbit of the moon and go beyond that line. This is the great gulf that is fixed between lives subject to death, and the deathless lives. It is this function of the moon that has given to her her sinister meaning in the minds of many, and it is also for this reason that she has been worshipped in the past as being the Keeper of the Gate, for she is indeed the Gateway between the realm of the mortal and of the immortal. It was in her function as the Moon Goddess that Isis dwelt behind the Veil, and to lift the Veil of Isis was the same as passing from the realm of mortality to that of immortality, it was for this reason that no Mortal had ever lifted her Veil. Before one can pass into that realm of immortality beyond the Veil, or rather in the act of so passing, one is born into immortality, and hence is immortal, hence only the immortals lift the Veil of Isis the Moon Goddess.

8. And all are full of Soul, and all are moved by it, each in its proper way; some round the Heaven, others around the Earth; [see] how the right [move] not unto left, nor yet the left unto the right; nor the above below, nor the below above.

And that all these are subject unto Genesis, My dearest Hermes, thou has no longer need to learn of Me. For that they bodies are, have souls and they are moved.

But 'tis impossible for them to come together into one without some one to bring them [all] together. It must, then, be that such a one as this must be some one who's wholly One.

And all are full of Soul, and all are moved by it, each in its proper way; some round the Heaven, others around the Earth, [see] how the right [move] not unto left, nor yet the the left unto the right; nor the above below, nor the below above.

The all here refers to all of the lives, or living things that we have been speaking of, both the deathless lives, and also the lives that are subject unto death. It is the sum-total of the lives that have been mentioned in the preceding paragraph of the text. The first statement in regard to them is that they are all full of Soul. This being true, there are none of these lives soulless, in other words it is not possible for such a thing as a soulless life to be. The next statement is that they are all moved by Soul. Now, that which is moved by another is a body, hence, all of these lives, whether they be deathless, or lives subject to death, are so many bodies, each of which is filled with Soul. It is the Soul within these bodies that energizes them from within, and thereby moves them. We then reach the conclusion that all lives, be they mortal or immortal, are bodies, there being no such thing as a life, in the sense of a living thing that is not a body. Even the gods then are bodies, filled with Soul, and moved by it. Without exception then, all the living things, all the lives of whatever order, are bodies, filled with Soul, and moved by Soul. But they are moved, each in its proper way. This means that all of these lives are not moved in the same way, but that there are ways proper to some of these lives that are not proper to others. This leads to the conclusion that there are diversities in the way in which the lives are moved, and that these ways of being moved, are in all cases, ways of being moved, proper to the lives that are being moved. This will mean that the lives have their individual movements peculiar to themselves. As it is Soul that moves all of these bodies, it will follow that Soul does not move all of them the same way, but moves each of them in accordance with its own proper way, hence the action of the Soul upon the several bodies, will be in accordance with the individuality of that particular body. This leads to the conclusion that Soul is in the lives, individualized in accordance with the individuality of the lives that it fills. Thus, Soul is not simple, but differentiated, and its differentiations are as the differentiations of the lives that it fills. One of these differentiations is into the two motions, one of which moves round the Heaven, and the other moves round the Earth. This refers to the two Zones of revolution if we may use the term: the Sub-Lunary, or the realm between the Earth and the Lunar Sphere; and the Trans-Lunary, or the realm beyond the sphere of the Moon. Understand that by the Earth we mean the Element of Earth that we have previously spoken of, and by the Moon, the Secret Moon that we have spoken of above. The Sub-Lunary Sphere will then be the sphere of Earth united to the transmutative Lunar Sphere, hence the lower matter of Cosmos. Heaven will be whatever is above this Lunar Sphere, the upper matter of Cosmos. Now, we are assured that there are two streams of these moving lives, one of which flows round the Heaven, and the other round the Earth. This means that there is a vast stream of lives flowing round the sphere of Earth, in the Sub-Lunary sphere, part of this stream passing through the Earth Element, and part of it passing through the Lunar World, a stream that practically fills both the Earth and the Moon, using both of these in the sense in which we have been using them all the time, as the Cosmic Matter in its lower sense, and as one of the seven subject Worlds. Another vast stream of these moving lives, is moving round Heaven, that is, moves through the space beyond the sphere of the Moon, completely filling that space which is here used as the equivalent of Heaven. Thus there is the Sub-Lunary and the Trans-Lunary streams of the moving lives. It will also follow that Soul belongs to both of these Zones, Soul being both Earthly and Heavenly in its nature, and thus energizing bodies in both the Earthly and the Heavenly realms, and moving them in the two streams, in accordance with the nature of the two that is within them. Also, we have another division in these streams of moving lives. Not only is there the Heavenly and the Earthly Streams of lives; but there is likewise, in both the Heavenly and the Earthly Zones, one stream that moves to the right, and the other that moves to the left. Those lives that are following the path of Construction and are revolving with the Cosmos, all move to the right. Those lives that are working in opposition to the revolution of the Cosmos, which are therefore, engaged in the work of destruction, all move to the left. We hear a great deal of twaddle about the Right Hand and the Left Hand Path. It is contended that one who pursues Occultism for his own advantage without reference to the welfare of others, is following the Left Hand Path, while one who pursues it for the good of humanity is following the Right Hand Path. In other words, altruism is said to be the Right Hand Path, while Egoism is said to be the Left Hand Path of Occultism. Now, all this is pure twaddle. Altruism and Egoism have absolutely nothing to do with the Right Hand and the Left Hand Path. The attitude one has toward humanity has absolutely nothing to do with it. One can not leave the Right Hand Path for the Left Hand Path, neither can he leave the Left Hand Path for the Right Hand Path. One never consciously chooses the Path that he will tread. The distinction is in the quality of the energy of the Soul-Stuff. If the Soul-stuff is such as to move to the right, then the lives will move to the right, if it be such as to move to the left, then the lives will move to the left. Now, observe this, the primary designation between the Right Hand Path and the Left Hand Path is merely in the fact that certain lives are in the right-flowing stream of lives, while other lives are in the left-flowing stream, we mean this as a literal statement of fact, and not merely as an ethical figure. Those lives that move in the right-flowing stream, are the one cooperating with the evolutionary trend of the Cosmos, while the lives in the left-flowing stream are working in opposition to the evolution of the Cosmos. It is for this reason that all lives moving in the right-flowing stream are among the ranks of the Builders; while all lives moving in the left-flowing stream are in the ranks of the Destroyers. Again let it be borne in mind that there are Gods, Goddesses, Demi-gods, Demi-goddesses, Daimones, Genii, Heroes, Souls, Spirits, Elementals and Elementaries alike on both the Right Hand Path and the Left Hand Path. Again, let it be understood that the Left Hand Path is just as essential to the Cosmic Evolution as is the Right Hand Path. The Right Hand Path and the Left Hand Path will both be found in both the Earthly Sphere and the Heavenly Sphere. These revolutions are continuous and never turn.

There is also the ascending and the descending streams of lives. The ascending stream is made up of the lives that are passing from the Earthly Sphere to the Heavenly Sphere, hence they are those lives that are filled with Soul the nature of which is to ascend from the gross to the subtle matter of Cosmos. The descending stream is made up of those lives that are filled with Soul, the nature of which is to descend from the Subtle to the Gross states of Cosmic Matter. In other words, the two processes of Alchemy are presented in the ascending and the descending streams of lives. They are the ones that are Ascending from Earth to Heaven, and the ones who are descending from Heaven to Earth. It is through these streams of lives that the transmutation and evolution of the Cosmos is brought about. There is, therefore, both the Ascending and the Descending Streams of the Life Wave going on at one and the same time. It is not true that there is an epoch during which all life is on the descent, and another epoch during which all life is on the ascent. The truth is that there is a perfect balance between the ascending and decending streams of lives, but that it is one class of lives that are ascending, and another class that are descending at a given time. As these two streams describe a spiral movement, it will follow that the ascending stream will ultimately reach the top, in which case, it will of necessity turn down and become the descending stream. In the same way, the descending stream will ultimately reach the bottom and hence it will be turned upward, and will become the ascending stream. Therefore, it is quite correct to speak of the upward and the downward arcs of the Line of Life, only we should bear in mind that there are Two Lines of Life, and when the Ascending Arc of the one reaches the Apex of its progress, it thereby becomes the Descending Arc, and likewise, when the Descending Arc of the other reaches the Nadir of its Descent, it is thereby turned upward into the Ascending Arc. The purpose of all this then, is not so much the development of the individual, as the transmutation of the Matter of the Cosmos. The individual will continue to ascend and to descend until such time as he has transcended the Cosmos. At the same time, even in his descent, he will preserve all that he has acquired in his ascent. These varying fates are experienced by all of the lives in the ascending and descending streams of lives. It is in this way that even the gods are not exempt from the Wheel of Birth and Death. It is all a part of the transmutation of the Cosmos as well as the resultant transmutation of the bodies and souls of the diverse lives.

And that all these are subject unto Genesis, My dearest Hermes, thou has no longer need to learn of Me. For that they bodies are, have souls, and they are moved.

We are next assured that all of these lives are subject unto Genesis or Becoming. This means that —none of these lives are permanent in their nature, but they are subject to Becoming, in the sense that they are changed from one state, in order that they may Become something other than what they were before. They do not remain the *same* but are changed to something *other* than their previous state. This, of course, applies mainly to the bodies rather than to the souls of these lives. Even the gods are subject to this Genesis. Change through Genesis and

Becoming is therefore the lot of all of these lives. Those on the ascending stream are changed from a lower to a higher state of body, through the action of Genesis, and likewise, those on the descending stream are changed by Genesis, from a higher to a lower state of body. It is in this way that they evolve in the line of their transformations on either the ascending or the descending arcs of their life stream. All of this has been seen by Hermes, through the aid of the Eye of the Mind, the Eye of Gnosis or the Eye of the Truth. He has realized all of this with this Sense that has come to him as a result of the unification of his own Sense with the Sense of the Mind. Mind then informs him that he has no longer need to learn from the Mind, seeing that he has experienced this Sight, which has rendered the totality of all the Cosmic operations sensible to him. He now knows all that can be known about the life of the Cosmos, and there is nothing that can be taught him on this score. He has attained unto the perfection of wisdom, and in this that has been said, there is the completeness of the Pleroma of the Absolute Truth in regard to the matter in hand. This perfection of Wisdom in regard to the life of Cosmos is summed up in this, all of these lives, whether they be mortal or immortal, are bodies, they have souls, and they are moved by the action of energy, that is by their being energized by the soul that is within them, and is there individualized as their own souls. As this is the last word in Cosmic wisdom, it will be well for us to examine what he says. In the first place we are to note that all of the lives in the Cosmos are to be viewed under three heads if we may use the term, they are all bodies, they all have souls, and all of these bodies are moved. There is in them no single element or characteristic that is not included in these three heads. There are then, no lives either mortal or immortal, except such as are bodies and have souls in the bodies, and likewise, there are none of them that are not moved by some other power apart from themselves. By this we mean that they are all of them passible to movement from without, and are not endowed with the power of self-movement. Let us first realize that all of these lives are bodies. This means that there can never be in all Cosmos, a single living thing that is not a body. It will be impossible for it to *be* in Cosmos unless it is a body. The gods are bodies, and so are the daimones, the genii, the elementals, the elementaries, the spirits and all the rest. All are bodies, but there is this difference between the mortal lives and the immortal lives, that whereas, all the mortal lives have compound bodies, compounded from the four elements, the immortal lives have composed, but not compound bodies. By a compound body we mean the compounding of the four elements in such a way as to produce something else than those four elements, but by a composed body we mean that the four elements are present in the body as being themselves and not as forming something else. It is this distinction between compound bodies and composed bodies that distinguishes mortal lives from immortal lives, their souls are the same in essence. While it is the soul that moves the body, acting within the body, yet this movement does not originate within the soul, but is rather a motion aside from the soul, that acting upon the soul, imparts to her the movement that in turn moves the body. These then are the three characteristics of all lives, both mortal and immortal, that they are all of them bodies, in which are souls, and that they are moved by some other motion acting through the souls upon the bodies, and the two kinds of lives are differentiated the one from the other, mortal from immortal by reason of the fact that the mortal lives have compound bodies; matter of the Earthly Sphere is compounded; but the immortal lives have composed bodies. The the Matter of the Heavenly Sphere is composed.

But 'tis impossible for them to come together into one without some one to bring them [all] together. It must, then, be that such a one as this must be some one who's wholly One.

He has indicated the diversity of the lives in Cos-

mos, but there is also to be taken into consideration the fact that Cosmos is one, and hence, all of the diversity of the lives in Cosmos are an unity. Seeing that Cosmos is itself Order, it must be that all that are in Cosmos are Cosmic, that is, Orderly, or subject to Order. If the diverse lives in Cosmos were not subject to Order, then it would not be Cosmos—Order, but on the contrary, it would be Confusion. In order that Cosmos may *be* Cosmos, it is essential that Order should be preserved in it, and in the lives that are in it. Now, these lives are diverse as to their bodies, and likewise diverse as to the individuality of their souls, also, they are diverse as to the way in which each of them is moved, at the same time, there is Order in the movement of the whole of them, so that in their entirety, they are a Cosmos Order. As they are in their entirety one, it follows that something had to bring them into this unity, seeing that in themselves there was nothing to bring them together into this unity. They are therefore brought into this unity, not of themselves, but by reason of something apart from themselves. This that brings them into one, must of necessity be the power that moves them all, and that works in the souls of all of them to move their bodies. Now, this movement that works in all of them to move them, moving them in such a way as to promote unity of movement, in order that it may move them so as to make of them an unity, must be in itself, wholly one, seeing that otherwise, unity would not determine its movements. The unity of the Sensible Cosmos then, will be the unity of something distinct from the Sensible Cosmos, and in this there must be no differentiation, but on the other hand, an absolute Unity. That which Moves the Cosmos then, as well as the lives in it, must be something other than the Cosmos, and likewise, it must be an Universal, as no Particular can do this. It will then have to be that which transcends Relativity and Particularity, hence something the nature of which is Sameness. It will also have to be something that transcends both Time and Becoming or Genesis, and likewise, it will have to be beyond the realm of body and soul alike. Thus we are able to see how it is that the Mover of the lives in Cosmos must be traced back through the working order in the Intelligible Cosmos into Æon as the Power and Energy of God, and how, in the last analysis, it is God that moves the lives in Cosmos, so as to make of them in their totality, an Order which is the Image of that Order that subsists in God Himself, and is made to exist in Cosmos as the Mirrored Image of God.

LESSON V

The Unity of Life

9. For as the many motions of them [all] are different, and as their bodies are not like, yet has one speed been ordered for them all, it is impossible that there should be two or more makers for them.

For that one single order is not kept among "the many"; but rivalry will follow of the weaker with the stronger, and they will strive.

And if the maker of the lives that suffer change and death, should be another, he would desire to make the deathless ones as well; just as the maker of the deathless ones, [to make the lives] that suffer death.

But come! if there be two, if Matter's one, and Soul is one, in whose hands would there be the distribution for the making? Again, if both of them have some of it, in whose hands may there be the greater part?

For as the many motions of them [all] are different, and as their bodies are not like, yet has one speed been ordered for them all, it is impossible that there should be two or more makers for them.

The argument that was introduced in the preceding paragraph of the Text is continued here. First of all, the many motions of all the lives in Cosmos are different. Second, their bodies are not alike, but all of the different kinds of lives have different kinds of bodies; yet, notwithstanding this, one speed has been ordered for them all. By one speed being ordered for them, we are to understand that the Order of the Intelligible Cosmos has ordered this speed, in the sense of forcibly establishing that speed in their movements. Do not be confused by this expression speed, it has the meaning of Rhythm or Wave Motion; it does not mean that the diverse lives move with equal rapidity, but rather that there is a certain wave of moving Force that carries all of the lives with it, something similar to the expression, the Life Wave in some Occult Literature. What he means to teach is that, far from these lives moving by reason of their own force, the Life Wave or Stream of Motion is in each of them, and they are moved by the motive power of that Wave of Motion, hence it is said that they all have one speed, that of the Life Wave. We may illustrate this matter by looking at the three motions of the Earth. The Earth revolves every day, likewise once a year, it completely revolves around the Sun, turning completely upon its axis, and once in a Great Year of nearly twenty-five thousand nine hundred years, it makes the circuit of the Twelve Constellations. Now, we may compare the motions of the diverse lives to the Diurnal Motion of the Earth, and the diverse streams of lives to the Annular Motion of the Earth, but this one speed of all moving lives to the motion of the Earth during the Great Year. Now, this one speed that has been ordered for all the lives, being the speed at which they are alike moved by the Force of the Æon through the Intelligible Cosmos, is in no sense influenced by the diversity of the bodies, or the diversity of their several motions, but acts upon them all alike, it must therefore, be something *other* than the composition of their bodies, or the motions of their souls, and as it is but one speed, and hence but one motion, it is impossible that there should be two or more such motions. This is true, because if there were two or more such motions, then they would move the lives in two or more diverse rates of speed. It must be that as they are ordered by but one speed, there is but one to order this one speed, hence there is but one maker for them, and not two or more makers, seeing that two or more makers could not order the one speed. If there be but one speed, it follows that but one speed has been ordered, and if this be true, but one Order is ordering them, and this being true, there is but the one Maker, ordering them with that one Order. Thus it will follow that there is but the one maker for them all.

For that one single order is not kept among "the many"; but rivalry will follow of the weaker with the stronger, and they will strive.

He means to say the many do not agree among themselves, but rather there is rivalry, and striving for mastery. He is teaching that there is no such thing as willing cooperation in the ranks of the many, but that each one wants the preeminence over some one else, and hence, there is perpetual striving, the one against the other. Therefore, there can never be any such thing as order grown out of the many. His idea is that when order is found among the many, it is not an order developed among them, but rather an order established among them by reason of a power greater than the power of the many, which forces the many to submit to it. Hence, the very existence of order among the many, demonstrates that they are controlled by some power stronger than they are themselves. We see here another illustration of the utter contempt which the Hermetic Logos has ever had for every form of Democracy. The Democratic idea is that the many will express their opinion, and what ever opinion the majority hold to, this will be accepted by the others, and all will be perfectly willing to yield their opinions and their wills to the opinion and the will of the majority. Now, as a matter of fact, such a condition is utterly impossible. The majority may agree on a certain course, and the minority, for fear of being assaulted by the majority, may submit to that course, but they are of the same opinion that they were before. Government is founded as a means of forcing the minority to submit to the will of the majority. It is for that reason that we have policemen and soldiers. The police power of a nation is the power that forces the individual to obey the laws rather than to follow his own opinions. Of course as a rule, the will of the majority is thwarted, because they elect men to office, who do not do what the people want them to do, but what they themselves want to do. Practical politics consists in the art of getting yourself elected to Congress to represent the majority, when you are in reality of the minority, and there enacting laws that are contrary to the wishes of the majority which you pretend to represent. There is never any such thing as the many reaching of themselves a common ground of action, there will in all cases be rivalry and strife. A policy never emanated from the masses. When they vote it is for the candidates rather than for their policies, it is the tendency of the biped sheep to follow leaders that enables a few men to govern them, hence all government is essentially Aristocratic and never in any sense of the word Democratic. He is holding that it is not in the nature of lives to agree, but that it is the nature of each one to seek the expression of his will, and in all of his relations with other lives, he will seek to dominate them. This is the nature of every one of the lives, hence, the many can never agree, seeing that it is a struggle in which each one is fighting with all the rest. This being true, order can never be established among the many if it has to come from the many. There can only be order among the many, when there is a will so strong that none of them can resist it, establishes its power over them, and coerces them all to obey it, and this must be the will of a single being. Autocracy must, therefore, be the only form of government capable of establishing order. He teaches, therefore, that the maker of the lives must literally make them obey him, otherwise there can be no order. Therefore, if there is order among the lives in Cosmos it is because the force of a single maker has determined their several courses, and they have not the power to do otherwise. In a word, none of them have Free Will but on the other hand, the wills of all of them are determined by a higher power than themselves. This is the Hermetic idea of the Cosmos, all lives are under the control of One superior Force, which they are unable to resist. Now the Hermetic Political Economy was similar to this. In the Hermetic view, the King is one in whom the Order of Cosmos is incarnate, to such an extent as to control all of the motions of his soul and spirit. In his case therefore, this Order takes the form of will, so that his will is ordered by the Order of Cosmos, hence he has the Cosmic will and not an individual will. Now it is to be borne in mind that in this view, will is the will-force, and not merely volition, the latter being an act of the will-force. We are then to understand that the Cosmic Order becomes will-force in the will of the King, and that he has no will in any other sense than this. The Majesty of the King. In this view the King is will-force, that impresses that will upon his subjects, to such an extent that their will is conditioned by it. In a word, his subjects are passible to the passion of the Royal Will. It moves them, and they are moved by it. The King's Majesty is that energy of his, by which and with which, his subjects are energized, so that they automatically express it in action. It is in this way that they are ordered by the Majesty of the King. In this view the King is never one of the people, but rather the focal point of the Order of Cosmos, a point in which all of this Order is focused, and where it becomes Majesty, or controlling will-force, which acting upon the people, conditions and determines their actions, so that the King is at all times obeyed. This power is the Majesty of the King. His Highness is that Higher Quality of his Life-force that gives him a greater dynamic power than any of his subjects and thereby enables him to transmute the wills of his subjects in harmony with his own. His Grace is that quality of his Force that enters into his subjects and thereby conditions them so as to make them better, not through fear, but through giving them a superior quality of will-force. Thus the King becomes a sort of god to his subjects, determining their conduct through the action of his Majesty, refining their qualities through the action of his Highness, and transmuting their will to a better state through the action of his Grace. Such men were termed Spiritual Kings because they ruled the spirits of their subjects and their bodies through their spirits. Such were indeed and in truth, Divine Kings. It is for this reason that Hermes contends that it is from the King that Order is established in a State. The order established by such a King, is a divine order, and is in no sense of the word human. It is such kings as these that can do no wrong, because their Majesty establishes order and justice among men. As the will of the King is not human but divine, it is at all times correct. At the same time it must be borne in mind that the people do not obey the King out of choice, but because they have no means of disobeying him, their conduct being determined by his Majesty. The subject, being energized by the Majesty of the king, acts according to such energizing. Whoever, has the Majesty to energize the people so as to determine their conduct is the King of those people, it makes no difference what name he bears. Thus it is that Order never originates among the many, but in every instance, it emanates from one, and enters into the many as individuals, ordering their conduct with its Order.

And if the maker of the lives that suffer change and death, should be another, he would desire to make the deathless ones as well; just as the maker of the deathless ones, [to make the lives] that suffer death.

He has indicated that a single order is never preserved among the many, but that, on the contrary, there will be rivalry and striving among them for the preeminence, hence a single order can come only from a single maker. Now, he goes on with the argument, and says, suppose there were two makers, one to make the deathless lives, and another to make the lives subject to death? What would be the result? Could they cooperate and thus work in harmony, each one doing his own work without interfering with the work of the other? Nay, the one who made the lives subject to death, would scorn the idea that the other maker was able to do a better work than he could do, therefore, he would not tolerate the idea that he should make the lives subject to death and then content himself to see his rival make more excellent lives. On the contrary, he would insist on making deathless lives as well, and would undertake to show that he could make lives superior to those his rival was able to make. Likewise, the maker of the deathless lives, would never be content to make them, and leave the work of making the lives subject to death, to his rival. He would say, as I have made the deathless lives, it of course follows that I have more ability in the art of making lives than has this rival of mine, who can only make lives that are subject to death. As the greatness of an immortal life transcends that of a mortal life, so does my greatness as a maker of lives transcend the greatness of this rival of mine, who can make only mortal lives, but is unable to confer upon them immortality. Therefore, he would say, I can make much better mortal lives than this rival of mine, therefore, he must stop this foolishness, and permit me to do all of the making. The natural rivalry between the two makers, would of necessity lead to two rival creations, and hence there would be eternal strife in the universe and hence no Cosmos or Order. Therefore, the fact that we have a Cosmos and not a Chaos, proves that there is but the one maker, of the lives subject to death and the deathless lives as well.

But come! if there be two,—if Matter's one, and Soul is one, in whose hands would there be the distribution for the making? Again, if both of them have some of it, in whose hands may there be the greater part?

Now the question of the two makers is reduced to the question of Matter and Soul as the two makers. Some might contend that material things, that is, bodies, were made by Matter unassisted by any other maker; and that souls were made by Soul, unassisted by any other maker. If this be the case; if Soul makes souls without reference to the bodies that are being made by Matter, and Matter makes bodies without reference to the souls that are being made by Soul, then in whose hands would be the distribution of Soul and Matter for the making? The difficulty is that if Matter followed her own caprice in making bodies, and Soul followed her own caprice in making souls, who would determine the number of souls that were made by Soul, and the number of bodies that were made by Matter? Is it reasonable to suppose that, each making without reference to the other maker's makings, there would be an exactly equal number of souls and bodies made? Would there not be the danger of souls being made for which there were no bodies, or bodies being made for which there were no souls? Or would there not be the danger of Matter making too many deathless bodies, and not enough bodies subject to death, or the reverse? And Soul making too many immortal souls and not enough mortal souls, or the reverse? You can see at a glance how complicated is the problem, and the absolute necessity of the work of Soul and Matter absolutely coinciding in the diverse types that they made in their work of making souls and bodies. But, what is to determine their doing this? What is to prevent a lot of work that is not in harmony and therefore abortive? Suppose this distribution is in the hands of both Soul and Matter, which exercises the greater control over the other? In either case, the one will be to an extent interfering with the other. Does Matter force Soul to make souls to suit its bodies? Or does Soul force Matter to make bodies suitable for its souls? We are absolutely forced to the conclusion that the distribution is not in the hands either of Soul or Matter, but that it is in the hands of some maker that is higher than either Soul or Matter, and one that is wholly One. Nay, rather are we forced to conclude that neither is Soul or Matter the maker, but rather that they are both used by the maker, Soul being the *materia* out of which he makes souls, and Matter the *materia* out of which he makes bodies, while he himself is above both Matter and Soul and is Ruler over both of them. This maker must be one who is wholly One, and who is able to express his Unity through the Duality of forces that he makes use of in his making.

10. But thus conceive it, then; that every living body doth consist of soul and matter, whether [that body be] of an immortal, or a mortal, or an irrational [life].

For that all living bodies are ensouled; whereas, upon the other hand, those that live not, are matter by itself.

And, in like fashion, Soul when in its self is, after its own maker, cause of life; but *the* cause of all life is He who makes the things that cannot die.

Her. How, then, is it that, first, lives subject unto death are other than the deathless ones? And, next, how is it that that Life which knows no death, and maketh deathlessness, doth not make animals immortal?

But thus conceive it, then; that every living body doth consist of soul and matter, whether [that body be] of an immortal, or a mortal, or an irrational [life].

There is as to their consistency, no difference between the bodies of immortal, mortal and irrational lives, in either case, if the body be alive, it is made up of soul and matter, the two must enter into it if it is to live. From this we are to understand that the constituent principles of the bodies of the immortals, of mortal lives and of the irrational animals are the same, they being made up of soul and matter. Hence, a god, a daimon, a genus, must have a body, and cannot live without it, and that body must be material. In like manner, a bird, a fish, a reptile, an insect or an animal must have a soul, and cannot live without it. All living things then must have material bodies and souls. There is here absolutely no distinction between them. A living body then is matter and soul in a state of union, that is matter ensouled by soul.

For that all living bodies are ensouled; whereas, on the other hand, those that live not, are matter by itself.

We are here distinctly informed that matter separate from soul can have no life, hence it is soul that makes matter to live. In a body of un-ensouled matter there will be no life, hence it follows that any living body, lives because of its soul. This shows that there is a soul in every living body, no matter how low in the scale of life it may be. The discussion as to whether the animals have souls or not is absurd, any living animal has a soul, and is alive because of its soul, whereas, a dead animal has no soul, and for that reason it is dead. To live is the equivalent of being ensouled, and likewise to be ensouled is the same as being alive. What ever lives then, is ensouled. There can be no life in matter separate from soul.

And, in like fashion, Soul when in its self is, after its own maker, cause of life; but *the* cause of all life is He who makes the things that cannot die.

By Soul being in its self, we are to understand Soul separate from Matter. Now, Soul while in this condition of separation from Matter is after its own maker, that is, in a subordinate condition to its own maker, the cause of life to bodies. That is to say, when Soul is joined to matter, it makes matter live by ensouling it. However, soul does not do this of her own volition, but under the compulsion of her maker, who is, therefore, the real cause of her ensouling matter and making it to live. The cause of all life however, the ultimate cause of all life is He who makes the things that cannot die. In other words, it is the maker of the souls themselves. He is the maker of the immortal lives, and through his making, bodies are made to live through their being ensouled by souls.

Her. How, then, is it that, first, lives subject unto death are other than the deathless ones? And, next, how is it that that Life which knows no death, and maketh deathlessness, does not make animals immortal?

Hermes introduces two questions here. First of all, how is it that lives subject unto death are other than the deathless ones? And second, if all lives are made by that Life which knows no death, and makes the deathless lives, why does it not make the animals immortal? Turning first to the first question: What is it that renders the mortal lives *other* than the immortal lives? Where is the line of demarcation to be drawn between the mortal and the immortal lives? What is it specifically that determines the mortality of the one, and the immortality of the other? We have seen how it is that all lives without any distinction whatever are composed of soul and matter; that all living bodies are such because matter has been ensouled, and that matter apart from soul is in all cases dead. This being the case, a mortal life has soul the same as an immortal life, and so does an immortal life contain the material body the same as does the mortal life. Now, seeing that they alike have bodies, and alike have souls; what is there in the life subject to death to determine its mortality? And in the deathless life, what is there to determine its immortality? There seems to be no distinction between them, what is it that constitutes one deathless, and the other subject to death. The second question renders the problem still more difficult of solution. A life is the result of the union of soul and matter, and of nothing else apparently, and they are the same in the case of both the mortal and the immortal life. Now, the maker of both the deathless lives, and the lives subject to death, is that Life which knows no death. Seeing that all the making is done by a maker who is Himself deathless, and who makes deathlessness, and is the maker of the deathless lives, how does He make the animals mortal rather than immortal. We have seen how it is that there is no distinction in the elements used, that is, soul and matter, now, if soul and matter are alike used by the maker of all lives; and if the nature of that maker is deathlessness, how can deathlessness, working through soul and matter, make some lives immortal and other mortal? How is it that the deathlessness of that Life enters into some of the things He makes, and not into others? This is the difficulty that is presented unto us, and it is essential that we should understand this; for if we understand this problem, we will have understood the essential distinction between mortal and immortal life; and thereby, will we understand the nature of the Gate between the two, and this is the most vital of all the questions connected with the Science of Alchemy. If there be some way by which we may bridge over the chasm between mortality and immortality, above all things, we want to find it out. If there is such a thing as Flesh Immortality to be attained, it will be through this secret that its attainment will be possible, and not otherwise.

LESSON VI

The One Maker of All

11. *Mind.* First, that there is some one who does these things, is clear; and, next, that He is also One, is very manifest. For, also, Soul is one, and Life is one, and Matter one.

Her. But who is He?

Mind. Who may it other be than the One God? Whom else should it beseem to put Soul into lives but God alone? One, then, is God.

It would indeed be most ridiculous, if when thou dost confess the Cosmos to be one, Sun one, Moon one, and Godhead one, thou shouldst wish God Himself to be some one or other of a number!

Mind. First, that there is some one who does these things, is clear; and, next, that He is also One, is very manifest. For, also, Soul is one, and Life is one, and Matter one.

The first proposition is that there is some one who makes souls and bodies, and who causes matter to be ensouled by Soul, that is, who directs the entrance of souls into bodies. The argument is that these are effects, and as there can be no effect without a cause, there must be some one who is the cause of Soul being individualized as souls, of Matter being formed into bodies, and of the entrance of souls into bodies. He has shown that these things are made, and there can be nothing made without some one to make it. To see the force of this argument, we must call to mind the fact that all things are bodies, have souls, and are moved. This movement is something independent of both the body and the soul, they are alike moved by something else, hence, there is some one to move them. This leads us to the conclusion that there is some one, who is neither Soul nor Matter, who does this work of ensouling material bodies and thus making them live. But, primarily he is directing his argument to the question of the making of deathless lives, and of lives subject to death. It is clear that both of these orders of lives are made, and if made, it is clear that there is some one to make them. Next, he undertakes to show that this one who makes these things is One. Soul is one, and Life is one, and Matter is one. Now, inasmuch as Soul is One, it must be that the one who acts upon Soul and dominates it must be likewise One, otherwise, Soul, under the control of many, would not act as an unity. So with Life and Matter, the fact that they both act as one, under the energizing and the control of the Maker, shows that there is an unity in the making, and hence the maker must be One in Essence to be One in Work. This indicates that who ever it is that makes these things, he must be one who is wholly one.

Her. But who is He?

This being granted, the question is: who is this maker, who is One, and who is the maker of Soul, Life and Matter, as well as of souls and bodies, and the ensouler of bodies by souls? He is not Soul, since Soul is His work. He is not Life, since Life is the result of His work in Soul and Matter: and He is not Matter; since He it is who transforms Matter into bodies which He makes to live. This maker, who is neither, Soul, Life nor Matter, but who uses them all, who energizes them through their passibility, this one to whom both Life and Soul are passible, who is He? It is evident that we must get back of the Sensible Cosmos to find Him. As the Cosmos is nothing else than the sum-total of all things made, the maker of these things is therefore, the Maker of the Cosmos, who then is this maker whose work is the Cosmos itself?

Mind. Who may it other be than the One God? Whom else should it beseem to put Soul into lives but God alone? One, then, is God.

Only God can put Soul into lives, because none other than He can control the action of Soul. Bear in mind it is not simply souls, but it is Soul as a Principle that He controls, and hence, He must be something higher and greater than Soul. We have previously seen that the Intelligible Cosmos is the orderly Work of Æon, hence that Cosmos would be merely the work of Æon in causing Soul to enter into lives, the work of making, but not the Maker. Æon is the Energy of God, the in-working Power of God, the force put forth by the Maker, which in its active workings, makes all things. God then is the Maker, Æon the energy employed in the making, Cosmos the work of making, Soul, Life and Matter the Material in which He works, in lives the finished product of His Work of Making. God alone can do this work. As this work shows Unity, it is of necessity the work of One Workman, seeing that an unity of work can only be consummated by One workman, hence this Worker is One, and as he is God, then God is of necessity One.

It would indeed be most ridiculous, if when thou dost confess the Cosmos to be one, Sun one, Moon one, and Godhead one, thou shouldst wish God Himself to be some one or other of a number!

Here the argument is based on the admitted Unity of all the works of God, and the conclusion is that if there is an unity in the works, it is logical to assume an unity in the working and hence One worker. Cosmos is One; but Cosmos is but the sum-total of all things made, and likewise the Work of God, hence this unity of Cosmos pre-supposes an Unity of God as the workman. Also, we find that every thing that He makes shows itself to be an

Unity, and of course the maker of that which is one, must Himself be One. This argument is based upon the contention that no two can be exactly alike, and therefore, no two workmen can possibly do the same kind of work in every respect, hence if there were two workmen making the Sun, their work would of necessity be somewhat different, and hence there would be a certain measure of inconsistency in the work that they did, hence the nature of the Sun would be Dual, not One. He is insisting that in all the Cosmos there are no duplicates, but rather that every single thing is individual, hence it is in its nature one. Now, the maker of such a diversified Cosmos, every single part of which is absolutely unique, must be One and not many. This is simply an elaboration of the argument that there is no such thing as a single order in the work of the many, but that a single order can only emanate from One, never from more than one. It is the continuation of the argument that we had in the previous lesson. The Godhead is Divinity as a principle. Now it is the contention of the Hermetic Theology that Godhead or Divinity is the Quality of God, just as Humanity is the Quality of man. If Divinity be the Quality of God or his Essentiality, and if this Quality or Essentiality be One, seeing that there are not two or more kinds of Divinity, but only one kind of Divinity, it follows that He of whom this Divinity is the Quality or Essentiality, must be one and not many. The argument then comes to this: the Quality and Essentiality of God is seen to be One, His Essence is One, His Energy is One, His work is One and not diverse, and whatever He makes is an Unit, so that all the things that He makes are so many Units, and likewise there is an Unity preserved in all of the things that He makes, taking them collectively, also, in all of his makings the Substance that He uses for making a certain order of things is One Substance; therefore, can we conceive of this God, who is the Esse of all this sequence of Unity as being Himself any thing but an Unity? Remember that Divinity is the quality derived from God, not the Esse of God previous to God. Can One quality emanate from many diverse beings? Diversity may come out of Unity, but it is certain that Unity will never come out of diversity. God then, must be Himself One. He can never be merely one of a number. The numbers grow out of the Unity but Unity never grows out of the numbers. In this way does he show the absolute Unity of God. Here however, we are likely to be asked; how then do you get the gods, if God is One? To this we reply that the Energy of God, in its energizings, must lose its Sameness, in order that it may engender Particular lives, hence it must become Particular and not Universal, otherwise, it could never engender the Particular. It is the Particularizing of the Sameness of the Energy of God that makes all Particulars. This Particularized Energy is in this way broken up into a number of particular Energies, each of which specializes a particular Quality, the Quality of each Energy being *other* than the particular Qualities of all of the other Energies, just as the Light of the One Sun is broken up into many diverse Rays, the Quality of each being diverse from that of the others, and yet they are all Rays of the One Light, but each *other* than all the other Rays, and likewise, *other* than the Inner Light anterior to the Rays. Now, these diverse Energies each with the Particular Quality, are the Great Supernal Gods. The Qualities of these Energies manifesting through Soul-substance are the Gods in Heaven. The Genesis of these Qualities in Spirit-substance are the Celestial or Spiritual Gods, and their motions in Matter are the Mundane Gods. Hence, as a matter of fact, there is but One God, but when His Divinity has become *other*, and has thereby lost its Sameness with His Essence, we term that particular Divinity the gods, indicating its Particular Quality by the name of a particular god. The One God is the Essence of all the gods, one of the Great Supernal Gods is the Energy of all the gods of that Ray; one of the gods in Heaven is the Quality of all the gods of that Spiritual Hierarchy of gods; one of the spiritual or celestial gods is the Nature of a given Band of the mundane gods, and a given one of the mundane gods is Determinism of a given Order of Mundane Life, the Genius of it so to speak. This will show how the Unity of the One God and the diversity of the ten times ten million gods are in reality one absolute Unity after all.

12. All things, therefore, He makes, in many [ways]. And what great thing is it for God to make life, soul, and deathlessness, and change, when thou [thyself] dost do so many things?

For thou dost see, and speak, and hear, and smell, and taste, and touch, and walk, and think, and breathe, And it is not one man who smells, a second one who speaks, a third who touches, another one who tastes, another one who walks, another one who thinks, and [yet] another one who breathes. But *one* is he who doth all these.

And yet no one of these could be apart from God. For just as, shouldst thou cease from these, thou wouldst no longer be a living thing, so also, should God cease from them (a thing not law to say), no longer is He God.

All things, therefore, He makes, in many [ways]. And what great thing is it for God to make life, soul, and deathlessness, and change, when thou [thyself] dost do so many things?

God is the maker of all things, but He makes them in many different ways, owing to the diversity of His energies. Seeing that he makes all things by energizing them, it follows that, if His energies be diverse, that which is energized will be energized in a diversity of ways, and hence there will be great diversity in the making of things, hence in the things that are made. It is because He does not come into immediate contact with the things that

He makes, but contacts them through His energies that are particular, that he makes particular things in many particular ways. He makes life, soul, deathlessness and change, or transformation through death, all these because He has certain energies that will work in all of those diverse ways. Some of His energies make things to live, others make them to be ensouled, still others make them to continue their living, and prevent their death, and still others cause things to pass through the change of death. It is in the diversity of the energies, energizing things in different ways that cause the differences in them. It is thus that we get the differences, not in the quality of soul, neither in the quality of matter composing the bodies, but in the quality of the energies by which both soul and body are energized. It is thus that the diversity in the things made is brought about, though God is One, Soul is One, Life is One and Matter is One, yet the diversity in the Qualities in the Energies with which the souls and bodies are energized, gives the diversity in the quality of the lives. And man should not be surprised at this diversity in the makings wrought by God, when he realizes that he himself makes or does so many different things. In this connection, doing and making are used as meaning the same thing. The theory is that to do is to make. To understand this, we must bear in mind the nature of action. Energeia is the in-working or activity, the action of which is energon, working in or energizing. Energy is then the energizing activity; it is energes, active, energetic to this end, which culminates in ergon or work. To do is, therefore, to work. The energy of a man is one that works in, and energizes, and its work is the act of working in and energizing, and to make is the result of this in-working, energizing work which is identical with action. Doing is therefore, the process of making that which results from such doing. Doing then is making, doing referring to the process of the working energy, and making referring to the effect of this upon matter. What we do is only accomplished in what we make. In all that man does, he is, therefore, a maker, and the complexity of his actions in that which he does, and that which he makes thereby, should indicate the complexity of the doing and hence the making which characterizes the energy of God.

For thou dost see, and speak, and hear, and smell, and taste, and touch, and walk, and think, and breathe. And it is not one man who smells, a second one who speaks, a third who touches, another one who tastes, another one who walks, another one who thinks, and yet another one who breathes. But *one* is he who doth all these.

The argument now takes up certain actions that are performed by a man, and undertakes to show that the energy of a man may express itself in diverse manners, and yet it will be the energy of one man who is doing all this. A man will see, speak, hear, smell, taste, touch, walk, think and breathe, and yet all of these actions are the actions of one man. If we look into this closely we will see the analogy of man's work to that of God, and also we will see how doing and making are practically the same thing. A man sees because of the activity of the Optic Nerve, by which light vibrations are communicated to the Sensorium, and there cause the production of the images of the things from whence they come in contact with the Optic Nerve. This is due to the fact that the Optic Nerve, and likewise the corresponding Center in the Brain are energized by a force connected with the Luminiferous Ether so that the image of the object may be produced in the brain, and hence in the soul. To see a thing, is to be energized by the Luminiferous Ether, and likewise to image it within, which is the same as to make its image within; hence, the act of seeing is identical with the making of the image of the thing seen. In fact what we see is the image and not the object, sight, therefore, is identical with imaging, which is both an action, and a making of the image seen; and this is the work of the energizing by the energy. Likewise to speak, is both to do and to make. To speak we must first form the idea with the reason, then we must express this idea in terms of the Fohatic Force of Sound within the soul, next the Sonoriferous Ether must be set in motion thereby, which acting upon the Vocal Organs, must energize them, and they acting in this way, will form the words as audible sounds. Thus speaking is a work, likewise it is an energizing and the action of the correct energy, the action on the physical organs as a result of their having been energized, hence it is a work done, and likewise, it is the making of the words. When you bear in mind that every word spoken lives for ever in the Sonoriferous Ether of Space, you will understand that words are both spoken and made. What I mean is that every word is a thing, and that every time a word is spoken, a brand new thing is created, and hence, speaking words, is the act by which we make those things which we call by the name of words. To make my meaning a little clearer, an unspoken word is subjective, but the moment it is spoken, it is made an objective word. It is for this reason that talking is such a great duty in the case of wise men, and such a crime in the case of fools. All ignorant men should have their tongues tore out, and all wise men should be forced to talk twelve hours out of every twenty-four. The reason is this, ideas subsist in the reason so long as they are unuttered. They may act within the souls of men, but they get no further. But the moment a word is spoken, the image of its idea is made in the Sonoriferous Ether of the Physical Plane, hence the Physical Plane is thereby taught the wisdom of the Logos. Hence men are to save the world in the sense of the Material Universe by talking. Of course this is the work of wise men, if fools talk, there is great danger of physical matter becoming as devoid of intelligence as they are themselves, which would be a great calamity. Hearing is the action of the Auditory Nerve, by which sound vibrations are communicated to the Brain, and thence within the consciousness. This is due to the fact that the Auditory Nerve is energized, and communicates the vibration of the Sonoriferous Ether so as to duplicate that sound vibrations within, hence it is the action of this energy, energizing the nerve and the inner being that produces the sensation of hearing, which is in reality the reproduction within us of that which is heard. It is the images of sound within that we hear, and to image that sound is to make its duplicate within us, hence, to hear a thing is both to do the deed of hearing and to make within us, the things heard, and it is through the energizing of the Sonoriferous Ether that this work is wrought. Smelling, tasting and touching is on the same order, the only difference is that we smell because of the energizing of the Olfactory Nerve by the Odoriferous Ether, which thereby communicates the vibration imparted to it by the soul of the odoriferous object to our own soul, which is the deed, and reproduce that same Odoriferous vibration in our soul, thereby making that same odor in our soul. In taste, it is the energizing of the Gustatory Nerve by the Gustiferous Ether, making the taste to be within us, as a sensation that energizes the soul. While in the case of touching, it is the energizing of the Tactile Nerves by the Tangiferous Ether causing the sensation by which the image of the thing touched is made within the soul, what you feel is the image in the soul, not the object touched by the body. Now, bear in mind that you cannot feel that image in the soul until it is there, and it has to be made before it is there, hence the deed of touching the object or of feeling it, is identical with the work of making its image within you. Take now the action of walking. It is no exception to the rule that we have shown rules over the other deeds of man. In walking, the first step is in the wish to be at a spot other than the one you are at present. This desire, in conjunction with the picture in the mind, sets in motion certain energies, with which the muscles of locomotion and the nerves of locomotion are energized. As a result of this, the muscles contract and relax in such a way as to move the feet. A step is made, as a result of that action of the limb by which it is taken. Now the point to be borne in mind is that the motion of the limb which is the deed, makes the step, and it cannot make the step apart from that action of the limb, neither can that action of the limb be done without at the same time, making the step. Likewise, it is to be borne in mind that this would be impossible without the corresponding energizing of the nerves and muscles of locomotion, just as we cannot energize the nerves and muscles of locomotion without that action of the limb that makes the step. In other words, energizing, doing and making are in reality three aspects of one and the same act.

Let us now take thought. When we think, the mind must first be energized by a particular energy. This energizing of the mind causes it to act under the stimulus of that energy, and a thought is made in the mind as a result of such energizing. There is then, the energizing of the mind, the mental action of thinking, and the making of the thought as a result of such thinking. Thinking is then three-fold; it is the being energized, the act or deed of thinking, and the thought made, and yet these are one process and not three distinct processes. Breathing is of like nature. The lungs are energized so that they as a result of such energizing, draw in the air, they extract from it a certain percentage of its Oxygen, pour into it Carbon, and other refuse matter, and expel it from them. Breathing then is accomplished as a result of the lungs being energized, and acting under the effect of such energizing, doing those things connected with the breathing, and at the same time, making the condition of body and of breath that results from such breathing. From the foregoing examples we can see how the life of man is made up of energizings, doings and makings, and that these are not three distinct actions, but rather three stages in one action. It in reality depends upon the energizing what the quality of the action is to be, and hence, it is the quality of the energy that determine the quality both of the doing and of the making as well as of the thing made. It is in this way that we are able to understand how it is that God does and makes all things through His energies, and their energizing of Soul and Matter. It may be stated here that the scope of man's life is determined by the number of his distinct energies, and by the diversity of ways in which he is energized. Likewise, the power of a man increases in proportion to the degree in which he is energized by his own energies, and decreases in proportion to the degree in which he is energized by his own energies, and decreases in proportion to the degree in which he is energized by energies apart from himself. The former state is seen in the energizing resulting in speaking, thinking and walking as well as in breathing, while the latter case is seen in the other actions that we have indicated above. Bear in mind that it is the one man who does all these, and that he does them through the diversity of his energies and their energizings, and so it is with God, He both does and makes many diverse things, owing to the diversity of His energies, in spite of the fact that He is One, that Soul is one, Life is one, and matter is one.

And yet no one of these could be apart from God. For just as, shouldst thou cease from these, thou wouldst no longer be a living thing, so also, should God cease from them (a thing not law to say), no longer is He God.

These actions on the part of man cannot be apart from God, seeing that all these actions are the result of man being energized by diverse energies, and the energies are not apart from God, seeing that all of the diverse energies are but differentiations of the Energy of God, seeing that there is no other source of energy save God. The Energy of God is the essentiality of all the energies, and hence they are His energies no matter how *other* they may have become, and how far they may have been transformed from their original Sameness. Thus all energies being but *otherings* of God's Energy, it follows that it is God energizing that energizes any thing at any time. This is all, therefore, evidence that God acts in all, and that whatever may be the immediate maker, God is the Ultimate Maker of every thing. Should man cease from his activity, by ceasing to be energized in the way that we have indicated, he would cease to be a living thing. This will give us the true nature of life. Man lives in his energizings, in his doings and in his makings. A man's life is in his seeing, speaking, hearing, smelling, tasting, touching, walking, thinking and breathing. It is this energizing, doing and making, that goes to constitute his life. Thus man lives in his activity, and not otherwise. Matter and Soul are alike Stuff. Man has a soul made of Soul Stuff, and a body made of Matter or Body Stuff, but he could have both a dead body and a dead soul, what is it that makes him live? Energy comes in contact with both soul and body, It is something distinct from both soul and body. but energy does not mean life until it does contact soul and body. Energy, soul and body while separate the one from the other do not give life. Life is then, neither energy, soul, or body, and it is not all three of these taken together. When energy enters into soul and body, they are energized thereby, and as a result of such energizing, activity is produced in soul and body, and this activity is Life, something that is never found apart from soul and body. Man's life is identical with his activity. The three factors in this activity are energizing, doing and making, and thus they together constitute the activity which is his life. But were his activities to cease, the man would be dead, and not alive. The degree of a man's life is, therefore, identical with the degrees of his activity, and not otherwise. To increase the measure of your life, it is only essential that you should increase the measure of your activities. The more active you are the more alive you are. From this you can see at once the utter fallacy in those who teach that one should shun activity, and seek a quiet inactive life if he would reach the heights. It is not in the quiet or retired life that one will find the highest measure of life, but on the contrary, it is in the most strenuously active life, that he really lives. It should be borne in mind that by activity we do not mean simply physical activity, but any form of activity, mental or otherwise. One may live in retirement, and still lead a very active life so far as the mind is concerned, and Concentration and Contemplation are in fact much more active than the most strenuous physical action. What we are in opposition to is the ideal of a quiet life rather than that of an active life. Man lives in his activities and in nothing else, it is this that constitutes his life, and in his activities does his life consist. This is the sense in which it is said that life consists in sensation. Sensation is the result of energizing, and of the activity resulting from such energizing, and the making growing out of such activity. To say therefore, that man lives in sensation, is merely another way of saying that he lives in his activities. In the same way, should God cease from His activities, He would no longer be God. God is the Energizer, and hence, He is God in so far as He energizes. His Life is in His activities, it is in them that He lives, hence were they to cease, His life would cease, He would cease to live. As He is God in His capacity as the Energizer, it of course follows that were He to cease to energize, He would cease His function as God, hence He would cease to be God. His Essence being to work, to do and to make through His energy, it will follow that were this to cease, He would cease to be God. This, however, is not law to say, seeing that if we admit the possibility of God ceasing from His work, we admit the possibility of His extinction, and this of course cannot be, seeing that all being depends upon the activity of God in His energizings, and therefore, it is not law to admit the possibility of God even for a moment ceasing from His activity, for it is certainly not law to suppose that God can ever cease from His Godhood, which would be the result were He to cease from His work of energizing all things. This goes to show that God can never be thought of as separate from Nature and the Universe. He is essentially the Workman, and the workman only is in the working and hence in that which he works, therefore we see the workman only in his work. God then is possible only in His work; therefore, God is to be found only in the Cosmos as His workshop and likewise as His work. Those, therefore, who would separate the Absolute from Relativity, Sameness from Otherness, the Unmanifest from the

Manifest, the Real from the Actual, and Reason from Things, have not understood the nature of Suchness, neither have they understood the Essence of God, Who subsists in the things He does and in the things He makes.

LESSON VII

The Divine Workman

13. For if it hath been shown that no thing can inactive be, how much less God? For if there's aught He doth not make (if it be law to say), He is imperfect. But if He is not only not inactive, but perfect, [God], then He doth make all things.

Give thou thyself to Me, My Hermes, for a little while, and thou shalt understand more easily how that God's work is one, in order that all things may be—that are being made, or once have been, or that are going to be made. And *this* is, My Beloved, Life; this is the Beautiful; this is the Good; this, God.

For if it hath been shown that no thing can inactive be, how much less God? For if there's aught He doth not make (if it be law to say), He is imperfect. But if He is not only not inactive, but perfect [God], then He doth make all things.

We have seen how there can be nothing inactive, for the reason that it is activity that constitutes the thing what it is. Matter is one, Soul is one, and Life is one, therefore, there is in none of these a single element of individuality or differentiation, hence only in their activities are things differentiated the one from the other. From this it will follow that the very being of a thing as being what it is, is its activity. In a word, the activity of a thing is its Suchness, it is the activity of a thing that constitutes it such as it is, rather than being something else. For this reason there can never be an inactive thing, seeing that it is the specific activity of the thing that constitutes it a thing, and that also constitutes it the specific thing it is rather than some other thing. It is in this way that we see that no thing can ever be inactive, as activity is the essence of things, just as inactivity would be the essence of *nothing* were it logical to speak of an essence of nothing. Activity is the same as being, while inactivity would be the same as not-being. Now, inasumch as this is true of all things, how much more is it true of God. How absurd would it be to say that the being of a thing depends upon its activity, but that He who brought this thing into being, who initiated its essential activity, is Himself inactive! It would be the same as saying that activity comes from inactivity, a statement that would be void of *sense* as well as void of intelligence. If there is aught that God does not make, then it has either been made by some one else, or else it has never been made, but is in itself Eternal. If it has been made by some one other than God, then the Maker of it is some one independent of God; but if it is Eternal and not made, it is independent of God. In either case, there is some one whose existence is not dependent on God, hence He is not supreme over all. And if there is any one, not subject to the will of God, then He has a limited jurisdiction, in which case He would be imperfect to that extent. Because God would be imperfect if there was any thing that was not dependent upon Him for its existence, it is not law to say that there is any thing that He has not made, seeing that to say so is to limit the perfection of God, something which it certainly is not law to do. But if God is not only not inactive, but perfect in the sense of being perfect activity, that is, as containing in Himself all activity, so that there is no activity save His alone, then He makes all things, seeing that there is no other activity apart from His to make any thing. God, therefore, makes all things, because His is the only activity and the only energy, He being the one and only Energizer. Thus God is seen to be the very Principle of Activity and Energy, and hence is He the Maker of all things made.

Give thou thyself to Me, My Hermes, for a little while, and thou shalt understand more easily how that God's work is one, in order that all things may be—that are being made, or once have been, or that are going to be made. And *this* is, My Beloved, Life; this is the Beautiful; this is the Good; this, God.

The injunction for Hermes to give himself to Mind for a little while, means that he is to surrender himself to the Mind, to become passive under its action, so that his own Mind may be completely energized by the Seed of Thought from the Mind, and thereby the consciousness of the Mind may be conceived in his own mind as being his consciousness. This is a state that can only be realized for a short time, ere one sinks back into the individual consciousness. God's work is one in order that all things may be one, that are made, that is that are being made at this time, or ever have been made at any time in the past, or that are going to be made at any time in the future. In other words, the unity of the made, depends upon the unity of the making, and hence upon the unity of the Maker. God Himself is One, His Esse is One, His Essence is One, and His Energy is One, seeing that His Energy is merely the in-working, energetic activity of His Essence. All this being One, it will follow that all of His working must be One, and as this working Energy is One, and as it energizes Matter which is one, it follows that all of His working must be One, and therefore, there will be an absolute Unity seen in all the work that He does. And it is this unity of His working, that causes all things to be. They are what they are because of the working of this Energy of God, and of that alone, seeing that there is nothing else to bring them into being. This is true not only of all the things that are now in process of being made, seeing that they are being made as a result of the present activity of His energy in its energizing of Matter; but it is also true of all the things that have been made in the past, seeing that there has never been any other energy to energize Matter and cause things to be; and likewise is it true that there never will be any other energy to energize Matter and bring things to be, hence God is the maker of all things that are ever going to be made at any time in the future. His is the only energy that can cause things to be, hence He is the only worker that ever has been, that is now, or that ever will be in the future. This is because His Energy is Æon, and therefore, in this Energy there is no such thing as Periodicity, but all its actions are spontaneous and present. This work, doing, making, creating, energizing is Life: for it is the Life of God, and it is its entrance into all bodies that makes them Live, and hence constitutes their Life. This is the Beautiful, for it is full of Beauty, this working and doing activity of God, for thus it is that the very being of God is perpetually being reproduced in action and in fabrication, and this is the very essence of Beauty. God's work is Beautiful because it is filled with His own Essence. This is the Good, for the Good is to give all, and God gives that which He makes. God's activity is the giving to that which is made, the energy that was required in making it, hence, whatever He makes, he gives to it, that of Himself which He places within it. He becomes that which He makes, and thus His Goodness is His making, hence His Goodness exists in His working and there alone. This is God, because it is in His work of making that He energizes with His energy, and His Godhood is His energizing, hence it is that He energizes in His making and in that alone, therefore, His Godhood is making, hence in His work. It is the Workman, the Maker that is Good, Beautiful and God; His working is His Beauty, His Goodness, His Life and His Godhood, and in nothing else do we find them.

14. And if thou wouldst in practice understand [this work], behold what taketh place with thee desiring to beget. Yet this is not like unto that, for He doth not enjoy.

For that indeed He hath no other one to share in what He works, for working by Himself, He ever is at work, Himself being what He doth. For did He separate Himself from it, all things would [then] collapse, and all must die, Life ceasing.

But if all things are lives, and also Life is one; then, one is God. And, furthermore, if all are lives, both those in Heaven and those on Earth, and One Life in them all is made to be by God, and God is it—then, all are made by God.

Life is the making-one of Mind and Soul; accordingly Death is not the destruction of those that are at-oned, but the dissolving of their union.

And if thou wouldst in practice understand [this work], behold what taketh place with thee desiring to beget. Yet this is not like unto that, for He doth not enjoy.

The word translated practice here is ergo—deed, work, hence Mind says "if thou wouldst in deed, in work understand this work, behold what taketh place with thee desiring to beget." He means that the deed present in the desire to beget, and the work would, therefore, cease to be, and as they would all by understanding one you will understand the other. By this he means to say that the work of God in making all things is a sexual work. That He does it as a Father rather than as a workman in the ordinary sense of the term; that He begets all things and makes them sexually. The meaning is that as He makes all things by energizing them, He in reality impregnates Soul and Matter with His energy, and thereby fecundating them, causes them to conceive and bring forth the things He makes, and that it is in that way that as a Father begets his children, so does God sexually make all things. It is in this way that we are to understand the making of things by God. He is the Father, and Soul and Matter are the Mothers of all things which are their children, begotten of God and born of Soul and Matter. Yet, there is this distinction, in the begettal of children, the father enjoys the sensations aroused in the sexual act, but God derives no enjoyment, and experiences no sensations in the act of sexually making or begetting things.

For that indeed He hath no other one to share in what He works, for working by Himself, He ever is at work, Himself being what He doth. For did He separate Himself from it, all things would [then] collapse, and all must die, Life ceasing.

In this paragraph we have the reason for what was stated in the previous one relative to God not enjoying in His making. He has no other one to share in what He works. Strictly speaking, God is both the Father and the Mother, the Husband and the Wife. Sexual enjoyment is due to the momentary union of two separate beings in the sexual act, and it is this moment of union that causes the enjoyment to both of them. In God, however, both the Masculine and the Feminine Principles are perpetually at-oned so as to be one being, therefore, the whole of the work is done by God alone, having no other one to take a share in it. This being the case there is in it, no enjoyment for Him. He works by Himself, there being no other activity entering into the work but His alone. He ever is at work, because the essence of His energy is to work, to energize, hence it is His very essentiality that He works. He has no motive in His work. He works for no reason, and to no end, but because it is the essentiality of His energy that it shall work, therefore, in His case, working is spontaneous. And likewise, He is Himself what He does, or makes. The meaning of this is that the very being of God subsists in this sexual making; for He is the maker, the process of making, and the thing made, all in one. God is only as the Maker, he could not be were it not as the Maker, and the Maker is maker only in the making, that is, in the process or act of making, and there can be no activity of making, without making something as a result of this activity; hence, what God does or makes is said to be Himself, for apart from it He could not *be*. Were God to separate Himself from His work or creation, all things would then collapse, seeing that they would no longer be energized, they would therefore cease to be, and as they would all die, Life would cease; for there would be no living things, and there can be no Life without there being something alive. In other words, there can be no such thing as Life in the Abstract. There is Life only because there is something alive. Life is activity, and there is no activity in the Abstract, but only is there activity because acts are being performed. Life, in the sense of activity, is only to be found in the sequence of acts performed by God. The activity of God makes all things, and He cannot be active or work, without making things; hence, were He to cease to make things His activity would cease, and His activity is His Life, hence His Life would cease and therefore, he Would die. The things God makes are the things he does, the making of things is identical with His deeds, and He is Himself what He does, that is, His activity. God is, therefore, identical with His work, and with what He does, for His Life subsists in His deeds. It is thus that God is so different from all other begetters, for He does not have congress with another, but with Himself alone, and His children are not born out of Him, but are made in Him, and He is in those He makes, and they are one, and are Himself.

But if all things are lives, and also Life is one; then, one is God. And, furthermore, if all are lives, both those in Heaven and those on Earth, and One Life in them all is made to be by God, and God is it—then, all are made by God.

All things are lives, because they are all active, and a life is an active thing or body; but a body is not a thing unless it is active. All differentiation is nothing other than differentiation of activity, therefore, all particular things are lives, hence all things are lives, that which is not a life is simply nothing, or the not-being. As Life is simply the activity that makes all things active, and hence makes them to live; and as it is activity itself, that is, unconditioned activity, it follows that there being no particularity in this activity it must needs be one, hence Life is one. And as activity is the activity of God, there being no other activity, then the oneness of Life means oneness in the activity of God, and as He lives only in His activity, it follows that His activity being Himself, He is also one. If as we have indicated, all things are lives, both those things that are in Heaven and likewise those things that are on Earth, if there is no exception, but they are all lives, and if there is in them all One Life, in the sense of one activity which is active in each of them, and this Life is made to be, that is, this activity is made active by God, in the sense of its being God's own activity or working, and God is Himself identical with this activity and hence this Life, then it follows of course that they are all made by God. God is the maker of all things, because it is the activity of God that constitutes that One Activity that is active in all things, both in Heaven and on Earth, which makes them live and is, therefore, their life; and as they are constituted as being what they are by their life, it follows that they are made to be by God, and hence they are made by God. They are both the deeds and the works of God, and in this sense they are made by Him and He lives in them. Thus all things both in Heaven and on Earth are made by God.

Life is the making-one of Mind and Soul accordingly death is not the destruction of those that are at-oned, but the dissolving of their union.

Life is the making--one of Mind and Soul in the sense that when Mind enters into Soul and energizes it, so that Soul becomes the passible matter energized by Mind as energy, Life results in the sense of Soul becoming active, and this activity established in Soul is Life. It is this that makes souls to live, and bodies too, through the joining of souls to bodies. Matter is made to live while it is united to Soul. Death is not the destruction of Mind as Mind, or of Soul as Soul, but merely the dissolving of their union, so that Soul is no longer energized by Mind, and hence the activity of Soul ceases, and it being no longer active is dead. Its inactivity being identical with death. The life of a soul, therefore, depends upon it continuing to be energized by Mind, and thereby kept active. It is the activity of souls that makes them live, and this activity depends upon the continuation of Mind's activity within them. The life of a soul will, therefore, be in proportion to the degree in which it is energized by the Mind as activity within it. The life of the soul can, therefore, be increased both in volume and in power unto infinity, simply by bringing the mind to bear more and more upon her, so that she is energized by mind to greater and ever greater degree. The mind must, therefore, become more and more active in the soul, so that it works in her, and she becomes to a greater and ever greater extent, the work of the mind, if we would realize the greatest possible degree of soul life.

LESSON VIII

Life and Death

15. Æon, moreover, is God's image; Cosmos [is] Æon's; the Sun, of Cosmos; and Man, [the image] of the Sun.

The people call change death, because the body is dissolved, and life, when it's dissolved, withdraws to the unmanifest. But in this sermon *(logos)*, Hermes, my beloved, as thou dost hear, I say the Cosmos also suffers change,—for that a part of it each day is made to be in the unmanifest,—yet it is ne'er dissolved.

These are the possions of the Cosmos,—revolvings and concealments; revolving is conversion and concealment renovation.

Æon, moreover, is God's image; Cosmos [is] Æon's; the Sun, of Cosmos; and Man, [the image] of the Sun.

Æon is the image of God in this sense; Æon is the Essence of God functioning as Energy; it is the Power of God in activity, the in-working activity of God in other words; hence, Æon is God as activity, the Divine Activity in fact. It is in this sense that Æon is God's Image, being the working activity or energy of God. Cosmos is the image of Æon, in the sense that Æon is the in-working, energizing principle, while Cosmos is the working of that energy, its energizing, and therefore, its activity, its work in the sense of the working which is the making. Thus Cosmos is Æon's image, in the sense of being what Æon is doing, Æon is energy, but Cosmos is the energizings wrought by Æon. God the energizer is imaged in Æon which is His energy, and this is in turn imaged in Cosmos as its energizing. But the Sun is the image of the Cosmos. By the Sun we are here to understand the first and highest of the seven subject worlds, the Secret Sun, which is identical with the Solar Energy of Heaven. This is the highest and finest of the forces of Heaven and therefore, of the Sensible Cosmos. The Intelligible Cosmos, which is the work of Æon, acts upon this Sun Substance, energizing it, and thereby causing to express in Time or Periodicity the working of the Intelligible Cosmos. In this way does the Sun become the image of the Intelligible Cosmos, in the sense of being *made* in accord with the making of the Intelligible Cosmos, so that the Sun is this same work, in the sphere of the Sensible Cosmos. Man is the image of the Sun in this way: the activity of the Solar Energy, enters into the soul of man, working in it, energizing it, and transforming it, so that it becomes the manifestation of this Solar Activity, becoming in fact the work of the Sun. These images are to be understood as meaning the reproduction in a lower substance of the activity of a higher energy. It means this and nothing else. We are, therefore, to understand that Man does not contain the Sun in his soul, but rather reaches up to the Sun, and is directly energized by it, while the other six subject worlds are in him. It is for this reason that Sun Worship, in the sense of the worship of the Secret Sun, is of such great assistance to man, seeing that thereby he renders his soul passive to the action of the Solar Energy, the energy that connects him with the Intelligible Cosmos.

The people call change death, because the body is dissolved, and life, when it's dissolved, withdraws to the unmanifest. But in this sermon *(logos)*, Hermes, my beloved, as thou dost hear, I say the Cosmos also suffers change,—for that part of it each day is made to be in the unmanifest,—yet it is ne'er dissolved.

Death is here stated to be identical with the dissolution of the body, and the withdrawal of life from the manifest into the unmanifest state. We are to understand that death in no sense means the cessation of life, but merely that life is now functioning in the unmanifest rather than in the manifest state. The only thing in death then is, the dissolution of the body through which life has been functioning, so that life, deprived of a body, must function independent of a body. Manifest life then is life functioning in a body, while unmanifest life is life fuctioning independent of a body. Now life, as we have seen, is activity, or energizing, hence there can be no life apart from this energetic activity, therefore, the dissolution of the body does not cause the energetic activity of life to cease. When body has been dissolved, the life ceases to energize in the manifest state, that is, through the instrumentality of a body, but becomes active in the unmanifest, that is, independent of any body, which of course means that the Matter in which it is active is in a state of diffusion rather than in the organized state. Do not be misled by what we say of Matter here, we mean simply the substance in which the life is active, the Static or Passible Principle in which the life is working energy. This then is the true nature of life and death. Life when taken in contra-distinction to death, means energetic activity within a body, and death means the same energetic activity apart from a body. Life then is life in body, and death is life apart from a body. Death is then life unmanifest, while what we call life is merely this same life in manifestation. There is no other distinction between the two. This is the true nature of change, the passing from the manifest to the unmanifest state of activity, and again the passing from the unmanifest to the manifest state of activity. It is thus that change from one state to the other is the transition between what men call life and death, but they are in reality but two aspects of one thing. Cosmos also goes through this change the same as does any other body. Each day a part of Cosmos is made to be in the unmanifest. There is, of course, no such thing as the dissolution of Cosmos as a whole, so that there is no longer a Cosmic body, but all the time, certain parts of the Cosmos are being dissolved as body, and their life is being restored to the unmanifest state, while other parts are being restored from the unmanifest state to the manifest state. The result is, there is always much of Cosmos manifest as there has ever been, and likewise, there is always as much of it unmanifest as ever. As this change is regular, there is the same portion of the Cosmos being dissolved as body, that there is coming into body, hence the Cosmos is ever passing through this change, and at the same time it is ever the same. No alteration ever takes place in the Cosmic body as a whole, and yet every portion of that Cosmic body is being changed.

These are the passions of the Cosmos—revolvings and concealments; revolving is conversion and concealment is renovation.

By passion we are to understand motion which moves that which is passible, the active motion. The passions of Cosmos are, therefore, the active motions of Cosmos that act upon the passibility of the matter of Cosmos. The two passions of the Cosmos are its revolvings and its concealments. Its revolving is its conversion and its concealment is its renovation. The concealment of the Cosmos is that motion of the Cosmic energy by which the separate parts of the Cosmos are dissolved as bodies, and are reduced to the unmanifest state. There in that unmanifest state, they are renovated and in that way prepared for a new appearance into the manifest state. The revolution of Cosmos is that active motion by which that which is renovated in the unmanifest state is converted into the manifest state of body. Thus it is that Cosmos is in its separate parts, forever being reduced to the unmanifest state where it is renovated, and then is being restored to the state of body, in this way is brought about the perpetual renewal of Cosmos, and yet the Cosmos as a whole is forever the same. This periodicity of renovation and conversion is the true essence of Time, for Time is nothing else but the periodicity of conversion and renovation. Therefore, Cosmos as to its separate parts, goes through the same changes of life and death that a man does, but owing to this fact, Cosmos is ever the same. Man entirely disappears because the dissolution of his body goes on as a whole, and not in its separate parts, while Cosmos being dissolved in its separate parts separately, remains in life as a whole. If man could acquire this art of being renovated and converted one Cell at a time, he would have attained unto the Cosmic life, and thereby he would have attained Flesh Immortality. It is because he lives and dies as a unit that he experiences death as he does, not because of any defect in his life, for his life never ceases at all.

16. The Cosmos is all-formed, not having forms external to itself, but changing them itself within itself. Since, then, Cosmos is made to be all-formed, what may its maker be? For that, on the one hand, He should not be void of all form; and, on the other hand, if He's all-formed, He will be like the Cosmos. Whereas, again, has He a single form, He will thereby be less than Cosmos.

What, then, say we He is?—that we may not bring round our sermon *(logos)* into doubt; for naught that mind conceives of God is doubtful.

He, then, hath one *idea*, which is His own alone, which doth not fall beneath the sight, being bodiless, and [yet] by means of bodies manifesteth all [ideas]. And marvel not that there's a bodiless idea.

The Cosmos is all-formed, not having forms external to itself, but changing them itself within itself. Since, then, Cosmos is made to be all-formed, what may its maker be? For that, on the one hand, He should not be void of all form; and, on the other hand, if He's all-formed, He will be like the Cosmos. Whereas, again, has He a single form, He will thereby be less than Cosmos.

Cosmos is all-formed in the sense that it has every possible form, there being no form that is not present in Cosmos. It does not, however, have forms external to itself, in the sense of there being a body of some kind in which Cosmos dwells as a soul in a body, it is not thus with Cosmos. We should not think of Cosmos as being energy working in matter which is distinct from it, or as being something inside of a larger body, for there is no extension beyond Cosmos, that is to say, there is no extra-Cosmic space, for all space is in Cosmos, there being no space beyond Cosmos. We must not think, therefore, of Cosmos as having a form or forms distinct from itself, as being out side of it, it is not thus that Cosmos is all-formed. Cosmos changes all forms itself within itself. This will be easily grasped when you bear in mind the nature of Cosmos. Cosmos is for one thing the work of Æon and the order of that work, that is, the order ordered by Æon. But, this working is not possible except as it is working in and through a medium, and this medium is Matter in a state of diffusion, that is Primal Matter or substance. Now it is this working into substance, this in-working and energizing of the Primal Matter that engenders all forms, hence, Cosmos being the in-working of energy in Matter, and the engendering of forms, it will follow that all the forms are engendered within Cosmos, and not external to Cosmos. All forms are, therefore, contained in Cosmos, and it is the space in which all forms move. Therefore, all forms are engendered in Cosmos, are dissolved and renovated in Cosmos, and are restored to their manifest state in Cosmos, and this is the sense in which it changes all forms in itself and of itself. It is both the maker of forms, their renovator, the substance of which they are formed, the energy that informs them, and likewise the space in which they move. This will show the especial manner in which Cosmos is all-formed. Seeing the manner in which the Cosmos is all-formed, and not destitute of a single form, but contains all forms in it, the question then is, what may its maker be? If Cosmos is itself and formed, and there is not a single form that is not in Cosmos, what way be the character as to form, of He who makes Cosmos to be all-formed in this way? If He is devoid of all-form, He cannot make that which is all-formed, for no one can make that which He is not himself. If the maker of Cosmos, is not all-formed or does not possess all-form He cannot make Cosmos and endow it with all-form, seeing that Cosmos is merely the work of His Energy, hence if Cosmos is all-formed, its character of being all-formed was worked into it by the working energy of God. That which is made to be all-formed, was made so by the making, of the Maker, and, therefore, that making is all-formed, and if so, the maker must Himself be all-formed as maker. On the other hand, if the maker is all-formed, He will be like the Cosmos which He has made, and in that case, He will in no wise be superior to the Cosmos. He has no one like unto Him, and therefore, He cannot be like the Cosmos, therefore, He cannot be all-formed. But, if He has a single form, He will be less than the Cosmos, seeing that as it has all forms, the single form of its maker will of necessity be one of the forms of the Cosmos, there being no other form for it to be. Therefore, we see that the maker of Cosmos cannot have a single form, as that would make Him less than the Cosmos; He cannot have all-form, for that would make Him like the Cosmos; and He cannot be devoid of all-form, for in that case He could not make the Cosmos to be all-formed; He is therefore, neither of all-form, of a single form, nor is He devoid of form. He is neither formless, many-formed, all-formed, or single formed. What then can be the maker of Cosmos as to His form?

What, then, say we He is?—that we may not bring round our sermon *(logos)* into

doubt; for naught that mind conceives of God is doubtful.

We seem to have reached a point where we know not of what we are speaking. God is not devoid of form, He has not a single form, He has not a number of forms, and likewise He has not all forms, this seems to indicate that He does not exist. We must find some definition of Him that will include all that we have indicated and will be perfectly harmonious with all of these statements. The mind cannot conceive any thing doubtful in God, for it is the very nature of the mind that in doubt it can conceive nothing, doubt being an act of the reason and not an act of the mind. To conceive God in the mind, means that the mind has been impregnated by the Seed of Thought from God, and therefore, whatever is conceived in the mind about God will be absolute truth, hence there can be no doubt in what the mind conceives about God. In the light of this it devolves upon us to find some interpretation that will give to us a definition of God that will be perfectly clear, that will harmonize all that we have shown as to the form of God, and that will leave absolutely no room for doubt as to exactly and specifically just what God is, and what His form is.

He, then, hath one *idea*, which is His own alone, which doth not fall beneath the sight, being bodiless, and [yet] by means of bodies manifesteth all [ideas]. And marvel not that there's a bodiless idea.

Idea is used in the sense of the root of form, and to a certain extent as the equivalent of form. An idea is in reality the form of a thought. The thought is conceived in the mind, and the reason informs it, and this rational form of the thought is the idea. It is the root of form in the sense that this ideal form, or form of thought is that initial formal expression that, acting upon Substance, causes it to assume form, and thus, the roots of all forms are to be sought in their ideas. To make the matter a little clearer, we may say that the idea energizes matter, as well as directing the course of the energizing, and thus it becomes the *norm* in a sense of the in-forming work in substance. Now, it is stated that God has one *idea* that is His own alone, that is, this idea is possessed by no one but God, there is no one else having such an idea as this. This idea of God does not fall beneath the sight, for it cannot be seen, it is in a word, not Sensible but only Intelligible; it is an idea that can be grasped by the reason alone, for it is a form of reason, not a form of matter. This idea has no correspondence in Matter, but is a form of the Logos, that is ensouled by Thought. This idea is bodiless, for it has no body, seeing that bodies are composed of matter, and this idea is not a form of matter but a form of thought. Nevertheless, by means of bodies, this idea manifests all bodies. The meaning of this is that all bodies have as the roots of their forms, ideas corresponding to the bodies of which they are the roots of form. There can be no body except as there is an idea, or ideal form engendered in the Logos, as it is acted upon by the Thought of the Mind. Such ideas, acting upon and within Soul, engender their respective forms, which acting upon Matter engender corresponding bodies. The ideas are in the unmanifest state, they are made manifest when they have engendered the bodies which are their sensible manifestations. Ideas then are the manifestors in bodies, and hence, they are the makers of bodies. It is through ideas that the work is wrought in Matter that makes bodies. The action of ideas then is the making of bodies. Now, this idea of God, manifests all ideas by means of bodies, though itself is without a body. It is then the idea that causes other ideas to be manifested by means of bodies. It is then the idea that directs the other ideas to energize matter, to work in it, and in this way engender bodies through which they may come into manifestation. It is the idea of renewal and revolution, the idea of manifestation and birth. It is the idea that determines the engendering of form and hence the coming into manifestation. It is, therefore, the idea to become informed, to appear and to become sensible, the idea to work and energize. This is the idea that determines the course of all the other ideas to inform. This then is a bodiless idea, an idea that never engenders for itself a form, that ever continues to be a form of thought, but never enters into Soul, hence never has for itself a soul form, much less a material body. In this sense, all other ideas are its forms, seeing that it is through the action of this idea that all other ideas have been informed as ideas from Mind and Reason, yet, it ever remains distinct from them, being what we might term the energizing idea, the work of which informs all other ideas. It is therefore what we might term to Idea of ideas. It is this because it causes all other ideas to be, being their idea, just as they are its forms, and it is also the informing process that informs these other ideas from Mind and Reason; at the same time this Idea, never becomes one of the other ideas, it never even incarnates in one of these ideas, using it as its form, hence, some one of these other ideas is never the form of this idea. And likewise, this idea is never contained in all of the other ideas taken collectively, hence they collectively are not the form of this Idea. And at the same time, there is nothing in any of these ideas that they have not received from the Idea of God, in the sense that they have been informed as what they are by the engendering work of this Idea. Hence, this Idea is not devoid of all that is in the other ideas. It is related to the other ideas as cause to effect. Therefore we should not marvel that there is a bodiless idea, for in fact, without such a bodiless idea, or root of form, there could be no other ideas, or roots of particular form, and hence no other bodies, seeing that it is the form of informing action that informs all the roots of form as ideas of things. It is the Idea of Ideas, just as all the other ideas are ideas of things. It is the root of root forms, just as they are the root form of forms. It is the form of forms, just as they are the forms of bodies. To every material body, there is a corresponding soul form, that energizes it, works in it, and whose work the material body is. Now, to every soul form there is a corresponding root of form, or idea, which is a form of reason, in the sense of being composed of Reason as the soul form is composed of Soul-Stuff, this root of form or idea in this sense, is the maker of the soul form, in the sense that this root of form, or idea works in the soul form, energizes it, and does it, that is, it is the deed of the ideal root of form that makes this soul form, just as it is the deed of the soul form that makes the material body. Now, in just the self same way, the Idea of God is the idea that engenders the ideas as roots of form, working in them and energizing them, doing them in the sense that its deeds, make the ideas as roots of form. But it is present in them only as active energy, it is its activity that makes them, hence it is the Idea of the making of roots of form, the Idea that determines the making of these ideas, and determines that they shall be roots of form. It however, is the idea in all of these ideas as roots of form, it is the idea for each of them, but is but one Idea itself. At the same time there is not so much difference here, for all the soul forms of a Type have but one Idea that energizes them all, and so do all the root ideas form a group of which the Idea of God is the single Idea. This Idea then is bodiless, for it enters into no bodies, seeing that they are all energized by soul forms. It enters into no soul forms, seeing that they are all energized by the roots of form, the ideas acting as such, but it enters into all the ideas using them as its forms, for it is the ideal roots of form that are energized by this Idea, hence it is without body, and without form, but it informs all the roots of form.

17. For it is like the form of reason *(logos)* and mountain-tops in pictures. For they appear to stand out strongly from the rest, but really are quite smooth and flat.

And now consider what is said more boldly, but more truly!

Just as man cannot live apart from Life, so neither can God live without [His] doing good. For this is as it were the life and motion as it were of God—to move all things and make them live.

For it is like the form of reason *(logos)* and mountain-tops in pictures. For they appear to stand out strongly from the rest, but really are quite smooth and flat.

This Idea of God or Form of God may be likened to the form of reason. Now, the form of reason is not one that can be likened to the form of a physical object, it must be conceived as being quite *other* than that. Reason must be thought of both as a noun and as a verb, that is, both as a thing, and as an action. As an action, reason is the process of activity by which a thought is in-formed as an idea. As a thing, reason is that principle or substance in which the thought is informed, and vehicled. Now, the form of reason is never to be thought of as a body, but rather as the process of activity by which thoughts are informed as ideas; it is the nature of the in-forming process by which thoughts assume the form of ideas. This is what we mean by an ideal form, we do not mean that it possesses shape, in the Geometrical sense, but rather a certain system of association, due to a given mode of energizing. This is what we mean by Pure Form, that is, form without shape. We very often speak of forms in a sense similar to this, when we speak of Forms and Ceremonies. In this sense by a form, we mean certain definite words, in all cases identically the same words, spoken in precisely the same relations, and never the slightest variation, either in the words used, or in the way in which they are connected. In a word, we speak of a form here as being the same as a given association of ideas. Now, take a Mantrum, this is a verse, composed of a given number of words, associated together, not with reference to the ideas which they represent, but with reference to the mathematical and vibratory value of the words used. These words are associated in such a manner that the numbers of the diverse words will all blend into a single number for the entire Mantrum, in other words, all the vibratory forces of the diverse words will blend into a single vibratory force, the nature and power of which is definitely calculated. It is for this reason that Mantra can never be translated from one language to another, seeing that their potency is not in what they mean as words, but in the potency of the blending of the sounds. A musical composition is an illustration of the same principle, it is a form of sound, as well as a form of vibration. In fact any form is in the first place, a form of vibration, for it is the vibration that moves the Atoms and Molecules into place, and in that way builds up the body. Now, realizing what is meant by a form of vibration, go back in your mind to the initiating of this form of vibration to that which is back of it, and you will see that these vibrations are the result of a corresponding association in idea that has produced this form of motion, and this is what we mean by a form of reason. An argument is also a form of reason, for it has a given number of ideas associated in a certain manner, and it is on this association of the ideas that the nature as well as the force of the argument depends. The process of reasoning is merely the process of constructing the form of reason. Refutation of an argument is the process of disintegrating the other man's form of reason. The Demonstrative Sylogysm is another form of reason, and a logos in the sense of a treatise or discourse is a form of reason, covering an entire subject. The process of reasoning is therefore, the process of building your ideas into definite form. It is for this reason that the reason is an absolutely infallible guide in the quest of truth. Synthetic reasoning is the process of building up a form of reason, through the natural association of ideas. By natural association we mean that association which the ideas seek of themselves, by reason of the way in which they have been in-formed by the reason. This we will call rational association, in contradistinction to volitional association, or that association which is brought about when the individual will or the influence of desire is permitted to determine the course of the reason. The function of analytical reasoning is to test the synthesis and ascertain whether or not the form of reason has been constructed through rational association, or volitional association, if the latter, then the form of reason is incorrectly constructed. What has been said will give you an idea as to the nature of a form of reason. It is in this sense that we must understand how it is that the Idea or Form of God is similar to a form of reason. At the same time it is to be borne in mind that it is this form or idea of God that acts upon the Reason so as to direct the in-forming of ideas, and thereby the association that goes on in the Reason. In other words, it is this Idea or Form of God acting upon and within the Reason that causes its process of in-forming thought as idea, and that likewise associates ideas into forms of reason. From this it will be seen that the form of God is simply a form of action, a form of Ideation, rather than a bodily form of any character.

Again, the form or idea of God is like mountain-tops in pictures. This is owing to the fact that they appear to stand out strongly from the rest of the picture, but really are perfectly smooth and flat. It is the way in which the paint is applied to the canvas that causes the mountains to appear in bold relief, and causes the tops of the mountains to appear as they do in nature. This is accomplished through shading, and through sharp lines in combination with the lines drawn for the purpose of shading. Lines are drawn in such a way as to be seen not as separate lines, but so that they present to the eye their common or general effect. It is the blending of these lines, so as to catch the light, and reflect it in a certain way, through their refraction of the light, that creates the illusion of uneven surfaces. Now, it is just in this way that the Idea or Form of God is to be understood. It is activity in the highest sense of the word, an activity which combines a multitude of distinct activities, in such a way as to blend them into a form of activity, which acting in Matter, that is the Primal Substance, refracts it by this activity, causing it to assume certain movements which are in reality the reflection of that diversity of activity in this form of activity, and thus is God pictured in the Cosmos. A picture is painted in permanent lines, in order that the shifting light, being refracted by those lines, may create an illusion in the consciousness of the observer, by the deception of the senses, appearing as a real mountain. In the Idea of God however, the lines are lines of activity, which acting upon the passible substances of space, refract that substance as active movement, causing the energizing of all forms and bodies through their senses. It is thus the Positive Picture, whereas the painting is a Negative Picture. This is the sense in which the Cosmos is the Picture of God, and it is in this way that the Ordering of the Cosmos by Æon is likewise the Adorning of the Cosmos. The Form of God is the mode through which He images Himself in the Cosmos. It is in this way that we are able to see how it is that God is not all-formed like the Cosmos, nor of a single form, nor yet devoid of all-form. His is the Ideal Form that becomes the Active Form in Cosmos, and this in turn becomes the material form in Matter. His is the ultimate Form of Thought and of Energy, Æonian in Essence and Life.

And now consider what is said more boldly, but more truly.

We have followed our logos up to this point, but we have not reached the ultimate depth of the subject as yet. We must consider it more boldly yet, and in this way we will strip the last thin veil from the Form of God, so that He will stand naked before us, and in this way we will arrive much closer to the truth than we have been able to reach by the reasoning that we have pursued up to this point.

Just as man cannot live apart from Life, so neither can God live without [His] doing good. For this is as it were the life and motion as it were of God—to move all things and make them live.

Obviously man cannot live apart from Life, we have shown that life is identical with activity, and hence, to live is identical with being active; therefore, our statement means that a man cannot be active without the action of activity. Living is Life in process of action, and therefore, without the process of activity, there can be no living, or Life is what causes a man to live. Living is the verb of which Life is the noun. Now, in this same way God cannot live without His doing good. Man lives in the activity of life that is going on in him, so God lives in His doing good. It is the doing good that constitutes the activity that is the Life of the continuity of God, for He is merely the doer of good. If we may use the terms in speaking of God, His life and motion are the moving of all things and the making of them live. The life of God is, therefore, the making of things to live, and apart from making things live, God has no life. We have seen how Life and activity are one and the same, hence, the activity of God is that which is active in every thing else, and which makes all things active. All things are merely the substance in which the energy of God acts, and it is this activity, specialized in the diverse forms that is their activity. There can be no activity that does not render something active, hence the activity of God is identical with the activity that makes all things active, hence His life is identical with that which makes all things to live. Doing good is merely the making of things to be. The activity of God acting in things, makes them active, that is, alive, and this is all that there is in doing good, it is that doing which is at the same time making. A deed is good in the sense that it is creative, it makes no difference what it is that it creates, if it makes something that was not existent previous to this deed, it is good. To do good is to make to live. God lives in the doing of good, in the making of things to be, that is to live, through the activity of His life, and it is only in that that

He lives. His motion is the moving of all things. Their passibility enables them to be moved by God, and it is their being moved by His activity that constitutes His motion, as well as their movement. Now, were there nothing to be moved, then He would move nothing, and if He moved nothing, then He would have no motion; for there can be no motion without something being moved; in which case He would be absolutely inert. Likewise if there was nothing to live, there would be nothing to make alive, hence God would not be making any thing to live, and as Life makes things to live, there would be no activity for His life to perform, and hence it would have no activity, therefore, it would not be active; and as a result it would not be life, in which case God would be destitute of life; and as that which is destitute of life is not alive, but dead; it would follow that God would be dead and not alive. As there can be no dead thing, and no inert thing, for it is action and motion that constitutes being, there would be no God. God, therefore, cannot be without the Cosmos of things, any more than it can be without God.

LESSON IX

The Master's Word

18. Now some of the things said should bear a sense peculiar to themselves. So understand, for instance, what I'm going to say.

All are in God, [but] not as lying in a place. For place is both a body and immovable, and things that lie do not have motion.

Now things lie one way in the bodiless, another way in being made manifest.

Think, [then], of Him who doth contain them all; and think, that than the bodiless naught is more comprehensive, or swifter, or more potent, but *it* is the most comprehensive, the swiftest, and most potent of them all.

Now some of the things said should bear a sense peculiar to themselves. So understand, for instance, what I'm going to say.

In philosophical discussions, we cannot in all cases use terms in the sense in which they are used in ordinary conversation. We are forced to give to the terms in ordinary use, a definite philosophical meaning which is quite other than the common meaning. This is due to the fact that it is not possible to find words that will express the subtle meanings which are expressed in philosophical discussions. In common usage, locatives in all cases refer to location in space, expressed in terms of extension, but if we wish to express certain relationships we must use locatives, but we will use them in a sense quite other than that of space and extension. This has forced all philosophers to develop a definite terminology, in which words in common use are given a technical philosophical meaning. They are the same words, but their meaning is vastly different. This is due to the fact that the vulgar mind thinks only in terms of the Objective Physical World, and hence, that which has no physical shape, has to such minds absolutely no meaning. Such people live in three-dimensional space, and hence, all their thinking is in terms of three dimensions, and no more. The philosophical mind, on the contrary, dwells in four-dimensional space, and hence, all the thinking of such a mind is in terms of the four dimensions. To the vulgar mind, things possess three dimensions, and hence, they are related the one to the other in their three dimensions, and not otherwise. They are in juxtaposition in their length, breadth and thickness, to the length, breadth and thickness of the other things, but the vulgar mind, thinking only in three dimensions, there can be no relation that is not one of the three dimensions. The philosophical mind, on the contrary, realizing that the three dimensions are merely so many phenomenal appearances produced to the senses by the action of the fourth dimension, thinks of the relations of things with reference to the manner in which they are related in their fourth dimension. The terms are used differently because of a difference in the association of ideas. The only ideas that the vulgar have are ideas of shape, and as they have no ideas of pure forms, they can have no ideas of the relations of pure forms, hence the vulgar thinking, and therefore, the vulgar use of words. Possibly we cannot indicate the difference better than to say that in vulgar usage, a word is the name of a thing, while in its philosophical usage it is the sign of an idea. As the philosopher thinks in terms of ideas, he speaks in terms of ideas, and therefore, whatever words he uses, represent ideas. The vulgarian thinks in terms of objects, hence speaks in terms of objects, and therefore, the words that he uses represent objects. This being true, the same word means to a vulgarian, an object, but to the philosopher it means an idea. From this it will follow that the two speak two entirely distinct languages, the vulgarian speaks the language of things, while the philosopher speaks the language of ideas. This will be true, although they use exactly the same words. This leads us to the distinction to be drawn between literal and symbolic speech. To the philosophical mind, words are the symbols of ideas, but to the vulgar mind, they are the names of objects. This distinction has enabled the wise to keep their knowledge from the vulgar, simply by speaking in the language of ideas, for the vulgar will never understand this, for the simple reason that they live in two distinct worlds. Many have found fault with us because we have not given our knowledge to the vulgar, but this was not possible. The vulgar could never understand what we were talking about, for the simple reason that to them, words do not mean ideas, but objects, therefore, we could not communicate our ideas to them, but would on the contrary, be naming objects, which we were not thinking about at all. For this reason it is utterly impossible for one of us to give a shred of our wisdom to the vulgar. We must leave him in his vulgarity, seeing that we have no means of expressing our wisdom in terms of his vulgar consciousness. We can never make wisdom vulgar, and therefore, we can never give of it to the vulgar minds. Therefore, we will have to confine our wisdom to the wise, that is to those having ideas, and hence understanding the language of ideas. It is in this light that we are to understand the statement that some of the things here said must bear a sense peculiar to themselves. We will, therefore, have to understand the definitions that are being given in the following instruction. Bear in mind that the words of the Text are used in the philosophical sense, not in the vulgar sense, that is, they are to be understood as being the signs of ideas, not as being the names of things. If you bear this distinction in mind, you will have no difficulty in following out the teaching.

All are in God, [but] not as lying in a place. For place is both a body and immovable, and things that lie do not have motion.

All are in God, but this is in a sense quite other than that in which we speak of something being in a given place, in the sense of lying in that place. They are in God, but are not there in the sense of locality, not in the sense of having a fixed location in space. Place is associated with body, and with that which is not moved. We cannot think of place except as we think of space in the sense of extension, and think of some particular section of that space, which never shifts its position. A body is in all cases something that is moved, something passible, that must, therefore, be moved through space by the motive power of energy. Now, we are not to think of things lying in a place, because in that case, they would not be moved, and it is in their being moved that they are bodies. Things that lie do not have motion, because it is due to the fact that they do not have motion that they lie, for lying is a condition foreign to the nature of the moved, and as all bodies are moved, otherwise they would not be bodies; it follows that bodies do not lie in places. The sense in which all things are in God is, therefore, quite other than this sense of lying in a place. We must seek in some other way for the manner in which things are in God.

Now things lie one way in the bodiless, another way in being made manifest.

There is, however, a sense in which things lie in the bodiless. Of course, it is a sense quite other than that in which they lie on the surface of a body; for they cannot lie in the bodiless in the sense of lying in a place, seeing that in the bodiless, there is no such thing as division into sections in relation to each other in terms of extension. In the bodiless, space is continuous, and not separated, therefore, to lie in the bodiless has a specific meaning, such as is not to be given to any other form of lying. And also, there is still another way in which things lie in the act of being made manifest. Ordinarily we associate the idea of lying with the idea of being continually in the same place, with immobility in fact. It is associated with the idea of a motionless lying in one position, we in all cases think of a thing as lying *still,* we never think of it as lying in motion; and yet there is such a lying as this, a perpetually moving lying. Another thing, it is difficult to conceive of a thing passing through change while it is lying; and yet this is exactly what we are dealing with when we speak of a thing lying in the being made manifest, in its condition of lying, it is changing from one condition to another, hence it is lying in change, or lying in Genesis. Lying then, is used here merely in the sense of the state of being something rather than another, the state or condition of being what it is, rather than being something else. Things are in God then, not in the sense of lying in a place, but rather in the sense that it is their vibratory relation to God that constitutes them what they are, they are in God in the sense of *being* rather than in the sense of location, they are in Him through Genesis, He being their *Esse.* They are in Him in the sense that their being made manifest is a being made manifest out of Him, seeing that He manifests them out of and from Himself.

Think, [then], of Him who doth contain them all; and think, than the bodiless naught is more comprehensive, or swifter, or more potent, but *it* is the most comprehensive, the swiftest, and most potent of them all.

We are not to direct our thought to God as Him who doth contain all things. We must understand the manner in which He contains them, for if we grasp this point aright, we will have mastered the entire secret of Cosmic Alchemy, and hence of all Alchemy as well. Let us first, however, try and understand the nature of the bodiless. What are we to think of the bodiless? What is to be our mental conception of it? In the first place, we must ascertain exactly what we mean by the bodiless. This does not simply mean the non-physical, or that realm where there are no bodies. In Hermetic Science, a body is anything that is moved by some force other than itself. Whatever does not itself, possess the power of self-movement, but is itself, passible to the action of another force, by the energizing of which it is moved, is a body. In this sense, souls are bodies, seeing that they are moved by the energizing of Æon. The bodiless is, therefore, that which is not moved by another force, that which is stable, and through which all bodies move, as well as that by which all bodies are moved. It is then the space through which all bodies are moved, and likewise the energy by which all bodies are moved; it is in fact very nearly identical with Æon. We must think of the bodiless as being the most comprehensive of all things, and that there is not any thing else any more comprehensive, for it comprehends all things within it. The bodiless must be thought of as the space in which all of the bodies are moved, there being not a single body that is not moved in this space. There is nowhere else for bodies to be moved, it is the *where* of all bodies. Likewise, we must think of the bodiless as being the swiftest of all things, and that there is nothing at all more swift than it. Swiftness relates to motion, and we are to bear in mind that all of the motion that there is, is in the bodiless, that is to say, not only do bodies move in this space, but likewise it is the space through which all of the moving currents of force pass. All the energies that move bodies must pass through this space in order that they may move the bodies that are in it. This means that all the energies are present in the bodiless, and there is not a single energy anywhere else. The bodiless is the space in which all bodies are moved, and it contains the energies by which the bodies are moved. Likewise, we must not think that there is any thing so potent as the bodiless, for it is the most potent of all things. Not only is it the space in which all bodies are moved, and the energies by which they are moved, but it is the One Energy, which is the potency of all those other energies, the working of this Energy is the principle of all the other energies, it is, therefore, the determinative principle back of all the energizings and movements, and this is of course Æon. In the bodiless are both potential motion and actual motion, and it is on this that every thing else depends. One must, therefore, completely change the mode of his thought. He must get rid of the superstition that the comprehensive, the swift and the potent are to be found in bodies, and must realize that they have none of either of these in themselves, but only such as has been put there by the bodiless, that all bodies are merely so many phenomenal appearances of the bodiless, that the bodiless is real comprehensiveness, real swiftness, and real potency. When we have learned to transfer our concept of the real, from the bodily to the bodiless, we will have arrived at the philosophical conception, and have forever abandoned the concept of the vulgar mind. But, there is another point involved in this conception of the bodiless, that we must not overlook. So long as you conceive of the body as being the comprehensive, the swift and the potent, you thereby awaken the energies in the body, and increase its comprehensiveness, the swiftness of its energies, and the potency of its magnetic force, such as can manifest as energies generated in a body, but you confine your life within that mold. You thereby render it impossible for life to manifest in you in any other way. Even though you think of your soul, so long as you confine in your thought, comprehensiveness, swiftness and potency to body, you will thereby sentence your soul to only that comprehensiveness, swiftness and potency that can be generated within it as a body, but you will separate it from the comprehensiveness, the swiftness and the potency that might enter into her from the bodiless. In the exact moment, however, that a man conceives truthfully the bodiless in his mind, he thereby connects his soul with the essence of the bodiless, with all of its comprehensiveness, all of its swiftnes, and all of its potency; and what is more, conceiving of his soul as bodiless, he completely merges it in the bodiless, transmutes it into essence, and thereby, makes it to become the comprehensiveness, the swiftness and the potency of the bodiless, so that it is bodiless itself, and therefore, is comprehensive of the comprehensiveness of the bodiless, swift with the swiftness of the bodiless and potent with the potency of the bodiless. In other words, to comprehend the bodiless with the mind, to conceive it in the mind, is to become the bodiless in the soul; to cause the soul to become in her essence, all that the bodiless is. It is for this reason that the conception of the bodiless in the mind is so very important; it means to conceive in the soul the bodiless state. This is the very essence of the Science of Alchemy, for in this way is the soul transmuted from body to essence, and hence from body to bodilessness. The passibility of body in the soul is thus transmuted into the comprehensiveness, the swiftness and the potency of the bodiless. This is the inevitable result of conceiving the bodiless in the mind, this conception will be born in the soul, as a bodiless soul essence, instead of a passible soul form, or soul body. The essentializing of the soul body is, therefore, the direct result of conceiving the bodiless in the mind. This is merely a case of freeing the mind from the influence of the senses, and causing it to think in the direct manner as mind free from sensation.

19. And, thus, think from thyself, and bid thy soul go unto any land; and there more quickly than thy bidding will it be. And bid it journey oceanwards; and there, again, immediately 'twill be, not as if passing on from place to place, but as if being there.

And bid it also mount to heaven; and it will need no wings, nor will aught hinder it, nor fire of sun, nor aether, nor vortex-swirl, nor bodies of the other stars; but, cutting through them all, it will soar up to the last Body [of them all]. And shouldst thou will to break through this as well, and contemplate what is beyond—if there be aught beyond the Cosmos; it is permitted thee.

And, thus, think from thyself, and bid thy soul go unto any land; and there more quickly than thy bidding will it be. And bid it journey oceanwards; and there, again, immediately 'twill be, not as if passing on from place to place, but as if being there.

This discipline which is here introduced, follows immediately on the instruction given in the previous section. To practice this discipline, one must have conceived in mind, the bodiless, and thereby, converted his soul into essence, an essence in which is manifested the comprehensiveness, the swiftness, and the potency of the bodiless. When one has attained unto this essential state of soul, he is then ready to enter upon the course of discipline indicated in the present section of the Text. Being in this state of essence of soul, through the conception of the true nature of the bodiless, think from thyself.

This is the exact reverse of the usual course of thinking. The average man thinks as a result of his soul having been energized by the senses. His physical senses are producing sensations that are imaged in his soul, and the soul being energized by those images of sensibles, generates what passes for thought. Such thinking is but the subjective response of the soul to stimuli from without, it is the reflex action of the soul under the action of sensibles. If he is on a somewhat higher plane of life, the senses of his soul will contact sensibles direct, and through sensation, these sensibles will be imaged in the soul, which being energized by these images of sensibles will produce that which passes for thought. The highest type is the one whose mind is energized by its sense, so that being directly energized by sense, it conceives thought direct. However, the mind in this case is acting under the stimulus of sense, and hence it is a subjective action notwithstanding that it is the mind itself that is doing the thinking. Even though the Seed of Thought comes direct from the Mind, or even from God Himself, it is still subjective thinking. We have to deal here with altogether a different order of thinking. To think from yourself, means that the thought is not the product of sense, that it is not the subjective reaction of the mind to energizing from without; but on the contrary, it is the direct energizing of the mind from within. Just as subjective thinking is the result of the impregnation and fecundation of the mind by Sense as Seed of Thought, so this aspect of thinking is the result of the self-impregnation and the self-fecundation of the mind by itself. It is in fact that power of the mind, by which its thoughts are turned inward, and made to impregnate it and conceive new thoughts. It is for this reason that only the enlightened mind can think from itself. In order that you may do this kind of thinking, the mind must have acquired a certain character or trend of thinking, a certain *nature,* which will enable its thoughts to reproduce themselves, without any seed of thought from without to impregnate it with their germ. When the mind has acquired this *nature* in accordance with which the thoughts are able to reproduce themselves, it is now able to spontaneously generate thoughts of a peculiar character or *nature* without any outside stimulation. This action of the mind is her direct action, in contra-distinction to the reflex action that we have seen to be the regular manner in which it acts. It does not react to sensation, but acts directly of its own power. This is only possible after it has conceived the bodiless, and no longer thinks of things as bodies. This is the true meaning of original thinking. Of course this would not be possible unless the mind had previously formed a concept or conception of the truth. It is for this reason that this discipline is never given until the correct view has been attained with reference to the nature of thought and of all things. In other words, the correct view of speculative occultism must be reached before the discipline in practical occultism can be given. Now, however, you are ready to think from yourself. This is done by conceiving thoughts in the mind as a result of her being impregnated and fecundated by her own thoughts, and by receiving these thoughts into the soul. They must not be permitted to leave you, and go out into space, but on the contrary, the soul must be made a receptacle for the reception of all of these thoughts, which entering into her, will there impregnate her with psychic states corresponding to the nature of these thoughts. It is this absorption of the self-generated thoughts of the mind, in the soul, and their conception of corresponding psychic states that is meant by thinking from yourself. It is in fact the establishing of the Subject, Predicate and Object of your thought alike in yourself. You are now master of yourself, in the sense of your soul being absolutely controlled by your own thinking, and that thinking being self-generated in the mind, without any action of sense. We are next told that you are to bid your soul go unto any land, and there more quickly than your bidding will it be. This has puzzled many commentators. Mead thinks that the text is senseless on account of this statement, and he is inclined to accept the reading of Patrizzi, who renders it "bid thy soul go unto India." This rendering is absolutely senseless and does absolute violence to the subject matter of the entire section. There is no reason why this should be given "bid thy soul go into India" any more than to bid it go to Australia or any other country. The teaching of this section is simply this: by thinking from yourself, you can render your soul Omnipresent. It is a discipline in Practical Magic, that and nothing else. What he means is this: thinking from yourself, in the sense of generating direct thought in the mind, let that thought enter into your soul, thinking that it is in any land that you may select, and imaging in your soul the thought of her being in that land. That is the sense in which you bid the soul go to some other land, you simply image in the soul, the thought of being in the land chosen. And there more quickly than your bidding will it be, means that when you have imaged in your soul, the idea of her being in such a land, she will immediately assume the character of being in that land. This is due to her having become essence, instead of being body. As she is essence, she simply blends with the essence of the soul of the land imaged in her, and as a result, she is identical with that essence, so long as she is imaged as being in that land. The statement that you are to bid the soul journey oceanwards is to be understood in the same way; it will be there immediately as a result of your imaging in it the idea of being on the ocean. We are informed that this presence of the soul in the locality imaged in her, is not as if passing on from place to place, but as if instantly being there. As we stated before, the soul is not as a body that has to be moved from one place to another in space. She is an essence, to which there is no such thing as space. Mind has entered into this essence, and it has become energized by its own energy, and thus does not have to be moved, but is vibrant with its own motion. It is no longer body, but is purely essence. Therefore, it does not have to move from one place to another, but, its essentiality is joined to the essentiality of the other place so that they become one in essence. It is in that place in precisely the same way that it is in God. From another standpoint, the place is in the soul, being joined to her essentiality, in just the same way that it is in God. It is the making one of the essentiality of the soul and of whatever one wished to reach, so that this place is essentially present in the soul, and is, therefore, not separate from the soul, but is in her, just as it is in God.

And bid it also mount to heaven; and it will need no wings, nor will aught hinder it, nor fire of sun, nor aether, nor vortex-swirl, nor bodies of the other stars; but, cutting through them all, it will soar up to the last Body [of them all]. And shouldst thou will to break through this as well, and contemplate what is beyond—if there be aught beyond the Cosmos; it is permitted thee.

We have here a series of statements relative to the powers of the soul, while following this discipline, each of which indicates a still greater power than the previous one did. First of all the soul may be present in any land at will, next it can cross the ocean by the exercise of this power alone. Now, one may bid his soul mount to heaven, and it will need no wings, and there will nothing hinder it, but borne on by this power of thought, it will be able to navigate the air, and even the aether of space, with nothing to interfere with it. This is of course merely a case of being wherever you think you are, or wish to be, merely visualizing your soul as being in such and such a place. You do not pass as a body from one place to another, but you are identical with that place, as to the essence of your soul. The fire of the sun will not do you any injury, but on the other hand you will be identical in essence with the fire of the sun, having its consciousness and absolutely being that very solar fire yourself. Neither will the boundless aether of space interfere with you; but you will be in essence identical with that aether, and hence being present as all of the aether of space, and not simply as being part of it, you will be it, essentially. The vortex-swirl will not interfere with you either. By this we are to understand the vortex or "whorl" of the solar system, see "Vision of Er"; also it is the vortex of a Circle, that is of the Cyclic Gods. This will not hinder you, but being essence, your soul will simply become that very vortex-swirl in essence, by reason of your imaging its idea in your soul, and expanding your thought beyond the vortex-swirl, imaging your soul as being greater than the vortex-swirl, your soul as essence will expand beyond it, and thus you will have transcended it. The vortex-swirl will be present in your soul, essentially, but your soul essence will be made to include other things as well. In this way, by imaging in your soul the bodies of the different stars, you become the bodies of all those stars, or rather they exist as bodies, in your soul which is the space in which they move, the essence in which they exist, and which is their essentiality. Thus you include all of the stars in your soul. However, the soul is not confined even to these, but it may soar up to the last Body of them all, that is to say, to the entire Sensible Cosmos as a body, becoming the essence of that Cosmos, so as to be identical with the Intelligible Cosmos; that is, the essentiality of your soul will be identical with the essentiality of the Cosmos, so that their essentiality will be that of the one essence, and the essence which is your soul will be that one essence. Hence, your soul will be the essence in which ever abides the Cosmos; it will be in you the same as it is in God. Your soul having become bodiless will be identical with the bodiless, and co-extensive with it, will contain the Cosmos within it, and will be the energy by which the Cosmos is moved and kept alive. But, you can even pass on beyond this state, and become identical with Æon, so that Æon will subsist in the essence of your soul. All this is possible, because the soul becomes in essence, identical with whatever the Mind thinks into it.

LESSON X

Æonian Life

20. Behold what power, what swiftness, thou dost have! And canst thou do all of these things, and God not [do them]?

Then, in this way know God; as having all things in Himself as thoughts, the whole Cosmos itself.

If, then, thou dost not make thyself like unto God, thou canst not know Him. For like is knowable to like [alone].

Make, [then], thyself to grow to the same stature as the Greatness which transcends all measure; leap forth from every body; transcend all Time; become Eternity; and [thus] shalt thou know God.

Conceiving nothing is impossible unto thyself, think thyself deathless and able to know all,—all arts, all sciences, the way of every life.

Become more lofty than all height, and lower than all depth. Collect into thyself all senses of [all] creatures,—of fire [and] water, dry and moist. Think that thou art at the same time in every place,—in earth, in sea, in sky; not yet begotten, in the womb, young, old, [and] dead, in after-death conditions.

And if thou knowest all these things at once,—times, places, doings, qualities, and quantities; thou canst know God.

Behold what power, what swiftness, thou dost have! And canst thou do all of these things, and God not [do them]?

What was stated with reference to the power of man in the previous section of the Text, is here called to mind. In view of what has been said, behold what power man has, and with what swiftness the soul is able to pass from one place to another, and if man is able to do all this, and to have all this power, why should not God have the same power, and be able to do the same things? It is to be borne in mind that the soul possesses these powers and this swiftness, owing to the fact that it is converted from body into essence. This means that while the soul is in the state of being essence, all these powers are perfectly natural to her. It is only while she is body that she does not possess them. Hence it will be perfectly natural that any essence shall possess them essentially. God being essence, or rather Esse, it of course follows that He possesses all such powers, within and of Himself.

Then, in this way know God; as having all things in Himself as thoughts, the whole Cosmos itself.

Here we are told exactly in what way we are to think of God, and what it is to know God. He is the Great Mind in which are present all things as Thoughts. It is in this sense that all things are in God. They are in Him, not as bodies lying in a place, but as thoughts conceived in a mind. Not as thoughts conceived in time, to pass immediately out of mind, but rather as thoughts permanently conceived in the mind, where they are permanent fixtures of the mind, ever remaining an integral part of that mind. This is in a sense somewhat like that of fixed ideas. Of course it is difficult for one to grasp this aspect of thought. Man is so prone to have all of his thinking spring from sensation, to think subjective, as a result of sensation induced by objects, that it is difficult for him to grasp the possibility of thinking of things prior to their existence. Nevertheless, it is in this sense that we must understand things being in God as thoughts. We must understand that they are His thoughts primarily, and that as a result of their being His thoughts, they become energies in Æon, which energies energize as Cosmos, and in this way all things are engendered from Matter. In other words, a thing is primarily a thought in the Mind of God; secondarily it is an energy of Æon; tertiarily it is a deed in the Intelligible Cosmos; quarterily it is a soul form, and quintererily it is a material body. This will mean that in Esse, all things are thoughts; in Essence, they are energies; in Action, they are Lives; in Form, they are souls; and in Appearance, they are material bodies. This being true, thought is the ultimate reality of every thing. A thing is really a thought, and only apparently something other than a thought. In God, then, things exist only as Thoughts; to Cosmos only as Ideas; and only in Time and Becoming do they exist as Things. For this reason, God is absolutely unconscious of things. He is even unconscious of their Ideas; and knows only their Thoughts, which are the same as His own thoughts. Now, to know God, we must know Him as being this, the Mind in which the Thoughts of all things perpetually subsist. So long as we think of God as being any thing else, we have not known Him. To God, the Cosmos does not exist as such. It is to Him, merely the Order of His thinking; just as particular things are His thoughts, so is the Unity of His Thought, the Order of Cosmos. Cosmos then is the Cosmos in the Thought of the Mind of God; simply that and nothing more. In a word, to Him there is no other Cosmos, save that of His own Thought. This Cosmos, as Essence is Æon, and in Activity it is the Intelligible Cosmos. In Time and Genesis, it is the Sensible Cosmos. Therefore, to God, there is nothing aside from or apart from Himself, all things *are* in His Mind as Thought; the Illusion that deceives others does not deceive Him. His Cosmos is the Cosmos of His Thought, and He has and knows no other Cosmos. Now, think of Cosmos then, as being as to its essentiality, Thought retained in the Mind, and as to its Actuality, activity, and as to its appearance, things. If you can realize this concept of Cosmos, you will understand the way all things are related to God, and the way they should be viewed by man.

If, then, thou dost not make thyself like unto God, thou canst not know Him. For like is knowable to like [alone].

Here we have the boldest, most daring instruction ever given to man. We have just been shown how it is that all things are in God. Now He is the Mind in which all things are present as thoughts; the Mind, the Order of Whose thinking, is the Cosmos, the Mind in the Thought of which is the Esse of every thing. Now, bear in mind, we have been informed that it is in this way that we are to know God. If we think thus of God, we will know Him. Therefore, being instructed as to how we are to know God, it follows of necessity that it is within our power to know Him, since we are told how we are to know Him. Now, in this paragraph of the text, we are positively told that unless we make ourselves like unto God, we cannot know Him. Like is knowable to like; but only the like is knowable. We can only know that which is like unto us. We cannot know God, unless we make ourselves like unto Him; but we can know God, He is knowable unto us; therefore, man can make himself like unto God. We have seen in what way God is to be thought of, and therefore, to become like unto God, is to attain unto that same kind of a mind. The teaching, therefore is, man must bring his mind into that condition where all things are present in it as thoughts. This means that the thought of the thing, as it subsists in the Mind of God, must be reproduced in the mind of the man, so that all the thoughts of God are present as thoughts in his mind. This is accomplished by thinking of thoughts, and not thinking of things. This is attained through a process of reasoning by which all things are reduced to their Ideas, and then, these Ideas are subjected to the minds, and through its action are reduced to the thoughts of which they are the forms; when they have been reduced to the initial thoughts in this way, they become permanently fixed in the mind, being imaged there, and becoming the *norms*, or molds of its thinking. This is possible, owing to the fact that the mental Cosmos of God is perpetually radiated as the Common Mind, and that Common Mind functions in connection with the soul of a man as his mind. The mind of a man is, therefore, capable of precisely the same Psychology as that of the Mind of God. In this way you are able to reach a state where all things as thoughts, subsist in your mind, precisely as they do in the Mind of God. In this way, you contain within you as thoughts, all of the ultimate sources of all things, hence you are all those sources, or rather they are your thoughts. Not only is this true of the thoughts of all particular things, but it is likewise true of the Cosmos as well. The thought of your mind, becomes a Cosmos which is identical with the Mental Cosmos of God, so that your thoughts are not separated the one from the other, but rather your thought is an unity, an Order which is a true Cosmos of Thought, and this is identical with the Cosmos of Thought which is the Order of the Mind of God. Thus the Mental Cosmos of God is present in your mind as its Cosmos of Thought. This being true, the Intelligible Cosmos will subsist in your mind as a Cosmos of Thought; hence, this Cosmos has no existence outside of you, but is all contained within your mind; it is not separate from you as an object, but it is present within your mind as thought. And this being true, there is nothing apart or distinct from you, but rather, all things are present in your mind as thoughts. Even God Himself is not distinct or separate from you; but even He is present in your mind as thought. It is in this way that you become All, and contain All within you, that is within your mind as thought. But, a point that is not to be lost sight of here is this: the soul being now essence, is acted upon as essence by your thought, so that whatever is present in your mind as thought, is likewise present in your soul as energy, therefore, all these things as well as the whole Cosmos, and God as well, are present in your soul, essentially, just as they are present in your mind, mentally. They are your soul, and your soul contains them all, as being parts of itself, and not as being possessions. It being essence, is identical with the essence of the Cosmos, and with the essences of all things. It is in this sense that you are able to know God, as being His very self in your self. As you have the same mind, the same thought, and the same essence, you are in this way made to be the *same* as God, and not *other* than God. Such a man may without blasphemy absolutely identify himself with God, and speak of God as I with perfect propriety.

Make, [then,] thyself to grow to the same stature as the Greatness which transcends all measure; leap forth from every body; transcend all Time; become Eternity; and [thus] shalt thou know God.

In this paragraph we are to see what follows as the result of what has been stated in the previous paragraph. In view of the *logos* in reference to the presence of all things in the mind as thoughts, man is instructed to make himself to grow to the same stature as the Greatness which transcends all measure. This simply means that after a man has mastered the Art of thinking the thoughts of things in his mind, and retaining their thoughts in his mind, so that they abide there as thoughts, his future progress is merely a process of thinking of things in this way, and of retaining their thoughts in his mind. There is no other problem involved, it is entirely a process of thinking, by which he retains the thoughts of all things, permanently in his Thought. At the same time it is a process, it does not become universal all at once. It is a discipline through which the mind must pass. It is not that one merely thinks of all things in general, the thought of each and every particular thing in existence must be specifically and individually retained in the mind. It is, therefore, a process of thinking of all the different things in the Cosmos of God, in such a way as to think their essential thoughts, that is, of each of them specifically. When this process has been carried on to Infinity, so that the infinity of the thoughts of things is in your mind, as the infinity of thoughts of things, you have reached the stature of the Greatness that transcends all measure. This of course means that you have in your mind as your thoughts, the Infinity of thoughts, and hence your mind is no longer finite, but infinite. It is to grow into Infinity of Mind and Thought yourself. The injunction to leap forth from every body, simply means that no body, no number of bodies, nor for that matter all the bodies that there are, taken collectively, will be able to contain that which is present in your mind. In other words, you not only contain in your mind as thought, all the things that have bodies, not only all the Species, but all the individual bodies as well; but you also contain in your mind the thoughts of those things that are without bodies, that is, the bodiless must likewise subsist as thought in your mind, not as being objective to your mind, but as being subjectively present in it, as its thought. You must also transcend all Time. Time here means Time as a Principle, that is to say, it is identical with Periodicity. Not only must all things be in the mind as thoughts, and not only that but the bodiless as well as all things functioning through bodies, but likewise, Periodicity itself must be in the mind as thought, that is to say, your thought must observe the Law of Periodicity, so that Periodicity of Thought will be in the mind. Time must be in the mind as thought, but also, the thought must go beyond all time, so that there will be in the mind, thoughts that are not subject to Periodicity, but which are of changeless and continuous quality. The entire Intelligible Cosmos must be in the mind as an Intelligible Cosmos of thoughts. But, in your thought you must reach even beyond this. You are charged to become Eternity, or Æon. This means that Æon must be correctly thought of, so that you have in your mind a mental energy that is exactly what Æon is. Your thought of Æon must be exactly what Æon is in itself. It must be Æon in thought, that precisely. This will establish Æon in your mind, and therefore, your thought will be Æonian, in fact it will be Æon. In this way does your thought actually become Eternity or Æon. By this, we mean that your thought is no longer periodical, nor even continuous, but is now simultaneous, so that in your thought there is neither past thinking, present thinking nor future thinking, but only simultaneous and Eternal thinking, an Eternity of thought in fact. Your thinking being Eternal, your thought is Eternity its very self. The result is, you have attained unto and have become an Infinity of thought, you are Omniscient in mind, Omnipotent in will, Omnipresent in soul, and Eternal in life. The quality of your mind is Omniscience, the quality of your thought is Infinity, the quality of your will force is Omnipotence, the quality of your soul is Omnipresence, and the quality of your active life force is Eternity. It is this which is meant by the attainment of Æonian Life. We must bear in mind that all of this Eternity is not only confined to the thought and the mind, but that it is an Eternity that is present in the reason as well, and hence your ideas are likewise Eternal. The soul being essence, this Eternity is in the soul essentially. Life being merely activity, your activity will be that of your energy in its energizing, and the soul being energized by this activity, which is Eternal, it will follow that your life will be Eternal also, hence, your life is now not only Immortal, but it has become Eternal or Æonian as well. It is thus that Eternal Life is realized in the soul. The will force, being the positive manifestation of this life force, which we have seen to be now Eternal, it will follow that your will is Eternal as well as your life. To all of this you will attain as a result of learning to think correctly from yourself. It is in this way that you may know God, seeing that you have become Æon, which is both the Essence of God and the Power of God; being, therefore, identical with His Energy and Power, and being that within yourself, seeing that that is now your life and your will, of course you will know God; He being of yourself, your self-knowledge will enable you to know Him. This will be a knowledge that will of necessity be Infallibly correct.

Conceiving nothing is impossible unto thyself, think thyself deathless and able to know

all—all arts, all sciences, the way of every life.

Having reached the lofty station which thought will bring unto you, the next thing is to reach the point where you conceive that nothing is impossible unto you. This conception is perfectly correct; for you now have infinity of thought, and with it, infinity of life and will, therefore, you have within yourself the power to create whatever you think of. Your thought is now creative, and hence, you only have to think of something in order that it may be. Whatever you think of as being, at once it is. Having this creative thought, the power of which knows no limit, it would never do to conceive that there was anything impossible to you; for, were you to think of something as being impossible, that thought would render it impossible, for it would prevent the thought of it from acting creatively through your power. You must, therefore, will create whatever you think, your condition you think of, and recognizing no bounds to your power, your thought will act as power, and therefore will create whatever you think, your thoughts will become things, no matter what the thoughts may be. You must in this attitude of thought, think of yourself as being deathless; for you are deathless only so long as you think of yourself as being such, seeing that it is your capacity to think Eternity that renders you Eternal; but so long as you think of yourself as being Eternal, you will be Eternal as a matter of concrete experience. Do not think that there is any knowledge that is beyond your grasp, for you can think all thoughts, and all knowledge is in thought; hence there is no knowledge that is beyond you, so long as you render your thought positive and creative. In this way, all arts are within your grasp. There is nothing that you cannot do, for you merely have to think the thought of what is to be done, and this thought will determine the action of your life and of your hand, so that at the first attempt you will be able to do it perfectly. There is no training at all needed, you merely have to think in terms of Art, and Art is at once accomplished. All sciences may be known at once in the same way. You do not need to study things, you only think their thoughts, and at once, all that pertains to them is conceived in your mind as thought. Take for instance, the science of Astronomy; the stars are all in your mind as thoughts, so that they are parts of yourself, you do not study them, you are merely conscious of what they are; you do not investigate them, you know them all most intimately. The way of every life, that is of every animal is known to you in the same way. Every life is in you as thought, and it is, therefore, in your life as a life, you know the way of every life, because through your thought and life, you are living the life of that animal just as he does. You know his life as the animal himself knows it. You do not study things objectively, you simply know them subjectively. It is a matter of consciousness and not one of investigation with you. All science is therefore, a part of you consciousness. To know a thing absolutely and infallibly, you merely have to think it. All knowledge is yours, because it is directly conceived in your mind through thought. You will in this way know things as they are and not as they seem, because you will know intimately that which causes them to be what they are, the determinative thought of them. One who has this mental capacity to know things in his own mind, can never make a mistake, whatever he thinks is absolute truth. This applies to the things of the Sensible Cosmos, quite as much as to those of the Intelligible Cosmos, it is as true of material bodies as it is Ideas; it cannot err. This infinite power of mind comes through the ability to think all thoughts, when this power is realized, all things are known because they are in you as thought and hence you are absolutely conscious of them in their completeness.

Become more lofty than all height, and lower than all depth. Collect into thyself all senses of [all] creatures,—of fire [and] water, dry and moist. Think that thou art at the same time in every place,—in earth, in sea, in sky; not yet begotten, in the womb, young, old, [and] dead, in after-death conditions.

The *logos* of this paragraph is the possibility of a man experiencing every conceivable condition of life, merely by thinking it. The idea is that one may think so strongly of a condition, that that condition will abide within his mind as thought; and the mind acting upon his life and soul, that condition as thought, will assume the condition of life, so that he will literally become that condition, so that he will experience the condition perfectly. The first injunction is to become more lofty than all height, and lower than all depth. Height and depth refer to the two extremes of vibratory activity, and the teaching is that merely by thinking of a condition as it is in its nature, the thought of that condition will establish it in the life of the one thinking of it. It is the doctrine of man's ability to think himself into any condition that he can think of. He can not only be at any stage of vibratory life, but he can think of the highest of all vibratory states in the entire sequence of vibrative life, and when he has thought of that, think of himself as vibrating more highly yet than that rate, and instantly he will be vibrating at a higher rate than any vibration in the Cosmos. He can reverse the process, and in his thinking, lower the vibration to the point of the lowest vibration in Matter, and thinking that, reaching it in his own vibration, he may then think of himself as vibrating still lower yet, and instantly he will be vibrating at a rate still lower than any vibration in the Universe. In this way, through the imaging of conditions in the mind through thought, a man can pass through the vibratory experience of everything in nature, and not only that, he can pass through vibratory experiences that nothing has ever gone through in all the history of Creation. In this way, a man can actually become something that never has been, as well as everything that has ever been. The entire scale of life and motion can in this way be actually experienced, and thereby known experimentally. Next, we are instructed to collect into ourselves all senses of all creatures. This means that by thinking of any and every creature, and by thinking of ourselves as being those creatures and of experiencing their senses, we will actually experience the sensations of all creatures and look at life as they do, we will literally live the life that they do, and go through exactly what they do, their Psychology will be ours for the time being.: Not only is this true; but suppose you wish to know exactly the condition of some age in the past? Suppose you wish for instance to know the life of the animals of the Tertiary Period? All you have to do is to think of some animal of that time, image him distinctly in your mind, think of yourself as being that very animal; and you will instantly possess the consciousness and the senses of that animal, and will pass through his experiences and live his life exactly as he did at that time. In this way, Geology and Paeleontology can be lived, in the sense of living the life of the time, and therefore, there will be no possibility of one making mistakes, your knowledge will be perfectly infallible. Again, suppose that you wish to know the state of society and of human Psychology say a million years ago? All that you have to do is to think of a man of that period, and think of yourself as being that man, think so strongly that that man is in your mind as thought, and you will actually go through all the experiences that he went through, you will be he in every sense of the word, and you will live his life exactly as he did at that time. You can in this way, know exactly what the history of the world was at any given time, not as one being told, but as one taking part in the making of that very history. As you have the power of being each and every one of those who took part in it, and not only all of them jointly, but each of the severally, there can be no possibility of your being mistaken. Not only can you live through the past, but in the same way, by the same power of thought, you are able to live through the future at any point in the future that you may wish to live. Not only does space cease to be a bar to your activity, but time as well, is a thing of the past, and all past, and all future time is something experienced at any moment through this power of thought. Not only do you have this power with reference to all animals and to men, but it extends to all plants and minerals, to fire, and water, and to the Dry and Moist Natures as well. You can become all elements, and pass through all the experiences that they do. In this way are you able to absolutely know all things, so that there is nothing at all that you do not know experimentally and hence perfectly. You do not have to be in different places at different times, but to you there is no such thing as space. Think of yourself as being Omnipresent, as being present in every place and in all places at the same time. Think of yourself as being so expanded that all places are in you, and that you are consciously in each and all of these places at one and the same time, in earth, in sea, and in the sky, and you will be there, and will consciously experience all that they experience, exactly as they experience it. At the same time, you can experience all the diverse stages of life in the experience of a man. You may do this either as a sequence of experiences, or you may experience all of these stages at one and the same time. Think that you are not yet begotten, and at once you will go through the exact experience of a child before it is begotten. Think of yourself as being the foetus in the womb, and you will experience the life of such a foetus, and that perfectly. Think of yourself as being young, and you will have all of this experence, you will be the child, and will pass through the experience of growing up. Think of yourself as being old, and all the experience of age will be yours, you will for the time being be actually old. Think of yourself as being dead, and you will experience all that the dead man experiences, you will lead the life of a dead man, and that literally and absolutely. Think of yourself as being in the after-death condition, that is, in the Spirit World, and you will pass through all of that experience, and will know that life, not as one going there in the Spirit and seeing the life of the dead ones, but as being one of them, and as living that life yourself. This knowledge and experience is due to the fact that by thinking of the condition, you actually create that condition in your mind, so that the condition is present in your mind as thought, and therefore, you are identical with that condition; so long as you think it, it is your own condition. All of these experiences are within the reach of man, either singly or all at once.

And if thou knowest all these things at once,—times, places, doings, qualities, and quantities; thou canst know God.

You must bring yourself to the point where you know all of these things at once, that is, are simultaneously conscious of them, and being them yourself. This must include the consciousness of all times, all places, all doings, all qualities and all quantities, that is to say, the consciousness of being them, and likewise the consciousness of what they are, in their inmost essences. If you have this consciousness of all of these, simultaneously present in your mind, you are then related to all of these things exactly as God is related to them. They are all in Him as thoughts in His Mind, and if they are all present in you as thoughts in your mind, then you are in the same relationship to them as is God; for that reason, functioning as God does, leading the life that God leads, having the same consciousness that God has, you are God for the time being, seeing that your mind is the same as the mind of God, and hence, you can in this way know God; because you know what He knows, and know it exactly as He knows it, being in the God Consciousness, by which we mean the Consciousness of God in the sense of God's Own Consciousness. There is no other way by which God can be known other than to function consciously with His Consciousness. It is in this way that man knows Him. To know God then is to have the same Psychology that is God's if we may use such a term.

21. But if thou lockest up thy soul within thy body, and dost debase it, saying: I noth-

ing know; I nothing can; I fear the sea; I cannot scale the sky; I know not who I was, who I shall be;—what is there [then] between [thy] God and thee?

For thou canst know naught of things beautiful and good so long as thou dost love thy body and art bad.

The greatest bad there is, is not to know God's Good; but to be able to know [Good], and will, and hope, is a Straight Way, the Good's own [Path], both leading there and easy.

If thou but sett'st thy foot thereon, 'twill meet thee everywhere, 'twill everywhere be seen, both where and when thou dost expect it not,—waking, sleeping, sailing, journeying, by night, by day, speaking, [and] saying naught. For there is naught that is not image of the Good.

But if thou lockest up thy soul within thy body, and dost debase it, saying: I nothing know; I nothing can; I fear the sea; I cannot scale the sky; I know not who I was, who I shall be;—what is there [then] between (thy] God and thee?

We have seen what it is that makes man like unto God, and hence, enables him to know God; we are now to find what it is that keeps this knowledge from man. We have seen to what a great station man may aspire, and the way in which it is to be reached; the question then is, why does not man reach that station? It is clearly evident that what we have said about man is not something that is realized in his experience; but rather the ideal state to which he should ever aspire: why then is it that men do not realize that state of life? It is now time for us to find out what it is that keeps him from this power and this knowledge. As it has been shown that man reached unto Æonian Life through a certain state of mind, through the power of thought; it becomes evident that it is the absence of this state of mind, and hence, the action of some other state of mind that prevents him from living the Æonian Life. The question then is, just what is that state of mind that will think man out of his Divine Heritage? The first statement is: if thou lockest up thy soul within the body. This means to confine the soul within the body, and limit it to the bounds of the body. This is accomplished by thinking that it is of necessity confined within the body, by thinking that the soul is something inside of the body; that the body is its dwelling place. This of course is the result of thinking that the soul is a body, the space of which is the physical body. By thinking of the soul as a psychic body, confined within the physical body, and unable to break beyond the limits of the physical body, you confine the soul to those limits, you make her to be what ever you think her to be. You are doing this thinking about the soul, so long as you think of her as a body and not as an essence. Every one is doing this who thinks of souls as space-filling, so that in a given space there will be room for only so many souls. To attribute size, in the sense of volume and Mass to souls, is to think of them as bodies, and hence, to deny that they are essence, and hence boundless, not subject to space, and not something to be moved, not passible, but self moving or rather all energy, all this you deny, seeing that you think your soul a body, therefore, by thinking it a body, you cause it to function as a body, and confining it within your body, in your thought, you actually lock it within your body, so that it can only function in that body. Another way in which the soul is locked in the body is by thinking that all knowledge comes as a result of physical sensation. If one believes that the soul acts only in response to the images that the senses make in her, of sensibles, then, so long as he continues in the belief, the soul will have to depend upon the senses imaging these sensibles in her. He will in this way, sentence his soul to depend upon the senses. The reason why the soul is whatever the mind thinks her to be, is this: mind enters into soul as an energy, and the functioning of the soul is the result of her having been energized by the action of the mind. The mind is active only in the act of thinking, hence, it is the thinking of the mind that energizes the soul, and determines the quality of life that will be manifested in her. Every thought of the mind is a distinct mode of energy so far as the soul is concerned. As a result, whatever the mind thinks about the soul, will energize the soul in that way, so that she is merely the active manifestation of whatever the mind thinks her to be. It is for this reason that the greatest difficulty in the way of realizing what we have shown to be the true station of the soul is this locking up of the soul within the body through the action of the mind, owing to what one thinks of his soul. The next great cause of individual limitation is the debasing of the soul, or the making of her small and of no importance. Humility is the greatest of all the vices. Modesty is the direct road to damnation. The mortification of self is the direct road to hell. The abasement of self will certainly lead to wreck and ruin. Instead of these, you must cultivate Self Esteem, the higher opinion you have of yourself the better. Remember this, you are in every instance exactly what you think you are, never more, and never less. You debase your soul when you think that you do not know anything. To take this view of the matter, is to deny to your soul the power of acquiring knowledge, and therefore, to deprive it of this power, to shut it off from all knowledge. To say that you can do nothing, is to deny that you have any power, and this means that power will not function in you. You thereby make your soul weak rather than strong. You are exactly as powerful as you think you are, never more, and never less. To deny your mastery over the sea and the sky, to admit in your thought that they are stronger than you are, is to make them stronger than you are. To think that you are subject unto the Laws of Nature is to make yourself subject unto them. Again, to say that you do not know who you were before your present incarnation, is to deprive yourself of the knowledge of that fact. If you think you know it then you do know it; for in the exact moment of your thinking you have such knowledge, you will become conscious of the knowledge. If you admit that the past is a closed book to you, then it is a closed book, for it is closed to you so long as you do not think you know it, and it is that opinion of your ignorance that keeps it closed to you. Think that you know all that has ever been in the past, and instantly you do know it. If you think that you cannot know the future, you do not know it, and you will not know it so long as you think that you do not. The moment, however, that you think you know all that will ever be in the future, you at once know all that will ever be. Now, inasmuch as the past recedes from the present to infinity, so that there was never a time when the past had its beginning, and as the future recedes from the present to infinity, so that there will never come a time when there will be nothing future unto it; it follows that there is in reality no beginning and no ending to time, in fact time is merely the Periodicity of Eternity, it follows that such a mind, knowing all past and all future events is in reality an Eternal mind; and when you realize that it is an Eternal mind, and think that your mind is Eternal, and includes all Eternity in its thought, at once this is exactly the condition of your mind and thought. But, if you deny to yourself all this, and assert that you are a weakling and have no power of any kind: what then is there in common between you and God? You deny to yourself all of the Attributes of God, and if you do not think you have them, then you do not have them, for you can have them only by thinking them into action in your own case. Such a man has nothing in common with God, there is not a single Godlike quality about him, and of course he can know nothing at all about God.

For thou canst know naught of things beautiful and good so long as thou dost love thy body and art bad.

We have seen how it is that all of the weakness of man is due to his identification of himself with his body, and thinking that his soul is also a body. It is the result of his thinking in terms of bodies. The difficulty then is that he has no mental conception of the bodiless. Not having this, he is able to think of nothing but bodies. A thing is either a body to him, or it is nothing at all. Thinking in all cases in terms of bodies, he has neither thought or idea of the bodiless. It is this state of mind that causes him to think of his soul as a body, and to energize it as a body in all of his thinking. Looking upon all things as bodies, it is natural that he should look upon his physical body as the most important part of his being. He is in grave danger of thinking that his body is himself. Now, the moment that he thinks that his body is himself, it promptly becomes himself to all intents and purposes, for there is now no functioning of the soul except through the instrumentality of the body. It is controlled by the body; and therefore, he grows into the position where he loves the body as being himself, he takes great pride in it, and most excellent care of it. This love for the body, draws all of the force of life into the body, so that there is no other energy save that which is active in the body. Life is active there and nowhere else, and therefore, he lives in his body, so that it is now in reality himself, seeing that he has no other life, in the sense that there is no other activity save that which is in the body. Such a man can know nothing of things beautiful and good, because all of his energizing is in his body, his life is active there alone, and hence he will be conscious of nothing aside from things of the body, the sensations and the thought that is engendered thereby. As the Beautiful and the Good pertain to the Bodiless, one who knows nothing but the body can of course know nothing of the bodiless, and hence nothing of things either beautiful or good. Being bad is here taken as practically the same thing as loving the body. Of course it follows at once that if one knows nothing of the Good, he cannot do any thing that is good. The doing of the good, is merely the result of active life, directed by the knowledge of the good. When one knows the Good, this knowledge of itself energizes his soul, and the active life is thereby made a sequence of active Good, that is, this knowledge in action, this is what is meant by living a good life, it is that your active life, not your deeds, but this life activity is engendered by the knowledge of the Good. This active life of Good, which is the activity resulting from the energizing of the soul by the knowledge of good things, produces actions, that is, it does deeds. It is in this way that all good deeds are performed. They are the deeds performed as a result of knowledge of Good energizing as life, and thus acting upon the body which is passible to the energizing of life. When the knowledge of the Good is absent, then it does not energize the soul with Good, and hence there is no active life that is the expression of Good, therefore, no good deeds are performed by a life activity that is not good. As there is no knowledge of the Good, the active life is the reverse of this, hence it is bad activity, and the deeds that it does are bad deeds, hence all that one does is bad and therefore such a man is bad, both in thought, in life and in deeds therefore, he will be entirely bad, so long as he does not know things beautiful and good. This will be the status of every one who loves his body, and thinks only in terms of bodies, he must be a bad man.

The greatest bad there is, is not to know God's Good; but to be able to know [Good], and will, and hope, is a Straight Way, the Good's own [Path], both leading there and easy.

We have seen how men become bad, we are now to see still more of the nature of this process of becoming bad. Of all the bad things, the greatest of all, that which makes bad more than all else, is simply to fail to know God's Good, or literally, the Godly or Divine. Good is the Esse of God as well as His Essence, therefore, to know God's Good is to know God essentially, to know His Quality or His Essence. The essential knowledge of God is, therefore, the same as the knowledge of His Good. Now, failure to know this is the greatest bad that is possible to man. The reason for this is not difficult to find. Whatever a man knows, dwells in his mind as thought, and only that which is dwelling in his mind as thought, does he know. To know God's Good is, therefore, to have God's Good dwell in the mind, as therefore, to not to know it, is not to have it dwelling in the mind as thought. If it dwells in the mind as thought, all the thinking of the mind is determined by that thought, so that the thinking of the mind is the thinking of this Good; but, if it does not dwell in the mind as thought, the thinking of that mind will not be determined by the Good, hence, such thinking will not be Good. If the thinking of the mind is Good, the soul will be energized by this good thought, and the life will be the activity engendered by this good thought, hence the life will be good. On the other hand, if the thought is not good, it will not energize the soul, and therefore, the life that is active, will not be the activity of Good, but will be the reverse, hence the life will not be Good. If the life is Good, it will express itself through the body in deeds, which will of course be Good, and therefore, the man will be Good in action, and hence a good man. If the life is not Good, it will act upon the body, and will act through deeds which will partake of the nature of the life that does them, and therefore, the deeds will not be good. The man being not good in action will not be a good man. That which is not Good is Bad, bad being the opposite of Good. To know God's Good is, therefore, to be a good man, and to not know His Good is to be a bad man. There are no exceptions to this rule. We see then what is bad, and the way in which one is a bad man. Let us, therefore, seek to know God's Good. The Straight Path is first to be able to know Good, by having the Good to dwell in the mind as thought, and next it is to will, that is for this knowledge of Good, or the Good dwelling in the mind as thought to be expressed in terms of will; for the thinking of the mind, being determined by the thought of the Good, to energize as will; and lastly it is to hope, that is, by the power of thought, seeing what is to be in the future, and concentrating all of the powers upon that state, make it determine what shall be. This means that the future state of our being becomes a fixed idea, that energizing the soul causes her to become what this idea represents. In a word, to become that which you will to be, and that which your thought tells you what you are, this is the true meaning of hope. This is pure Alchemy of the highest order. It is that power by which you become in deed and in action what you are in thought. This truth was known and taught in the Bible, in the New Testament in particular. We read "these three, Faith, Hope and Charity, but the greatest of these is Charity." And no one has ever dreamed while reading these words that he was face to face with a statement of the Alchemy of the Soul. Faith is exactly what we have been talking about; the holding of Divinity in the mind as thought, the mental conception of the Good, so that it is present in the mind as thought; Hope is the energizing of the soul with this thought so that the thought becomes active as life, and hence the activity of the Good thought in the soul as her life; Charity is the expression of this Hope in deeds, so that it is Divinity in action. No wonder then that it is said that Charity is the greatest of all; for Faith is Divinity of thought, Hope is Divinity of activity or energy; but Charity is Divinity in active, practical life, Divinity in Work so to speak. This Straight Way is the Good's own Path, that is to say, it is the course pursued by the Good, the current of the Good in its energizing, hence to pursue this Path is to do exactly what the Good, or Divine Essence does in the Work of God. It is to work as God does, to share in His Art of Creation, uninfluenced by any thing else. This is, therefore, to be freed from all the influences of Cosmos, to be greater than Fate. This Path leads directly to this state of Goodness, so that one pursuing this Path becomes perfectly and purely Divine, in every sense of the word. It is the easy Path, for it is perfectly natural for one who enters this Path to become Good and Divine without effort on his part. What we mean is that one pursuing this Path will without effort on his part, simply by thinking, willing and hoping, without any other effort, become perfectly and absolutely Good. By Good we mean the Essence of God, His essential Divinity. This is the station that is reserved for the man who follows the Path of the Good, and there is no possibility for him to fail in reaching the goal that he has started out to reach.

If thou but sett'st thy foot thereon, 'twill meet thee everywhere, 'twill everywhere be seen, both where and when thou dost expect it not,—waking, sleeping, sailing, journeying, by night, by day, speaking, [and] saying naught. For there is naught that is not image of the Good.

As soon as a man has entered on this Path of the Good, as soon as he has set his foot upon it; which means as soon as he has joined in himself, the Good as thought in his mind, as power in his will, and as activity in hope, so as to become life or action in the soul; as soon as in this way he has set his foot upon the Path, the Good will meet him everywhere. He will not have to seek the Good, but everywhere he will find that and nothing else. He will in fact cease to live in a world of bad, and will actually live in a world where there is nothing but the Good. Everywhere you will see it, and it alone. In such times and places as you would least expect to find the Good, there will it be seen. Whether you be waking or sleeping, sailing or journeying in some other way, whether it be by night or by day, whether you be speaking or keeping silent, in all times and in all places, under whatever circumstances you may be placed, you will see and experience the Good and the Good alone. For, seeing that the Good is within you, your life will be determined from within, and not from without. The reason for this is in the fact that there is nothing that is not an image of the Good. Being able to see this as truth, the man on the Good's own Path, looking into every condition that he contacts and seeing the Good imaged there, holds it in his mind as a thought, and one that is Good, so that in his mind every thing abides as being Good, to him it is Good. What we mean is, such a man does not recognize the thing as a thing apart, he recognizes only the thought of it, and that thought of the thing, he keeps in his mind as Good, therefore, it is Good in his consciousness of it. This means that such a man dwells in a word of thought, and to him, things are thoughts, and as thoughts they are all Good. He sees all things, therefore, as essence, and living in a world of essences, all things are Good. Such a man sees things in their reality, not in their appearances. He is in the position of the Three Wise Monkeys, one of whom has his eyes closed to evil, the second of whom has his ears closed to evil, and the third of whom has his mouth closed to evil. The meaning is, "if you think no evil, you will see no evil, you will hear no evil and you will speak no evil." In this way, the man of whom we are speaking, thinks only the Good, hence he sees only the Good, he hears only the Good, and whatever he speaks is Good. To such a man, the bad is simply non-existent. He is conscious only of the Good, and as that only exists of which we are conscious, therefore, there is only the Good, and there is nothing Bad to such a man. We do not wish to be understood as teaching that this applies merely to his interior life, we mean that as a matter of fact there is nothing but the Good so far as he is concerned. In his world there is nothing but the Good, and therefore, the Laws of Nature are non-existent so far as he is concerned. It is this which renders him superior to the laws of Nature. Nature does not apply to him, his thought is the only force that energizes him, and as his thoughts are all Good, it follows that he leads a perfectly Divine Life in practical things as well as in the interior life. Having the Divine Nature and not the Cosmic Nature, such a man is possessed with Divine Power in all that He does. He is indeed the Master, who is subject unto nothing but his own thought.

22. *Her.* Is God unseen?

Mind. Hush! Who is more manifest than

He? For this one reason hath He made all things, that through them all thou mayest see Him.

This is the Good of God, this [is] His Virtue,—that He may be made manifest through all.

For naught's *unseen*, even of things that are without a body. Mind sees itself in thinking, God in making.

So far these things have been made manifest to thee, Thrice-greatest one! Reflect on all the rest in the same way within thyself, and thou shalt not be led astray.

Her. Is God unseen?

So much has been said of the nature of God, of Mind and Thought, of Æon and of Cosmos as Work, that one is likely to look on all of this as merely abstraction, something that can be grasped by thought, but is beyond the reach of Sense. Hermes is lead to think that this must be the quality of God, something that we can think of in the mind, but have no ability to Sense, and therefore, that God cannot be approached through Sense. He, therefore, asks whether this is true or not.

Mind. Hush! Who is more manifest than He? For this one reason hath He made all things, that through them all thou mayest see Him.

The answer to this is that we may see God through His manifestations. If you will call to mind what has previously been said about the manner in which God is made manifest, this will be seen at once. The Power and Essence of God is Æon; therefore, we are to think of Æon only as being the essence and the Power of God, which is essential energy. The Intelligible Cosmos is merely the Order of the Activity of this Energy, this Energy working. The Sensible Cosmos is merely this working energy energizing through souls and bodies, this energizing being Life. Now, if we look at the matter in this light, all things are but so many manifestations of the working of the Energy of God; hence they are all manifestations of God. To do is to make, and therefore, all things made, are identical with things done, hence all things are merely so many deeds or acts of God. One can, therefore, see the activity of God in the things that are made by that activity. They are what they are because they are energized in the way that they are, and they are energized in that way on account of the activity of the Energy of God; therefore, a contemplation of the things made will show the way in which God's Energy works. In this way can one see the Quality of God in the work that He does, the Workman can be known through the knowledge of His works. As all things are the works of God, and hence the workings of God, He is manifest in them; and as we can see those things through sense, we are, therefore, through sense, able to know what God is, and thus we are able to see God through the exercise of sense. Hence God is clearly not unseen, but is most distinctly seen through the medium of His Work.

This is the Good of God, this [is] His Virtue,—that He may be made manifest through all.

By saying that this is the Good of God, he means that it is in this that God's essential Divinity consists, that this is His Esse as God. His Godhood depending upon it. The saying that it is His Virtue, or Strength, His Potency, means that God lives and is God in the act of doing this. It is in His being made manifest through all. In other words, the essential Divinity of God is in this, that He Works, and therefore, expresses or manifests His own Esse through the Work which is characteristic of His Essence. It is the Essential Divinity of God to Work, it is His Virtue to Work, and on this His very Being depends and for this reason is His Godhood manifested in the Work which He does, in what He does, and hence in what He makes. This being true, we can see in all things the manifestation of the Divinity of God. As this is the case, Sense will enable us to see God as Worker, which is His essentiality.

For naught's *unseen,* even of things that are without a body. Mind sees itself in thinking, God in making.

Even things that are without bodies are not unseen, though of course we do not see the things without a body with our physical senses, but there are senses with which we may see the bodiless. Here we get a view of the senses in which sight is used here. Mind is seen in thinking, that is, we are conscious of the act of thinking, and through the act of thinking, we become conscious of mind, that which thinks. God is seen in making, and likewise He sees Himself in the act of making. We are made conscious of the process of making, by reason of the things made, there can be no things made, except as a result of the process of making them; hence, in the thing made, we are conscious of the process of their being made, and through this, we are conscious of the Maker of those things, hence do we become conscious of God. We see, therefore, that seeing is here used in the sense of becoming conscious.

So far these things have been made manifest to thee, Thrice-greatest one! Reflect on all the rest in the same way within thyself, and thou shalt not be led astray.

In the things that have been made manifest in this logos, we have the key by which all things may be known. The Law as it were is here given, and no matter what it is that one wishes to know, by the application of the mind to the problem in accord with the principles of thought that have been given in this logos, one will not err. To be mistaken is utterly impossible if one follows the order of thinking that we have indicated. His thinking must of necessity lead him to the absolute truth in reference to the subject of his thought. The principles that we have given will not only enable one to find the truth on any and all subjects, but they will likewise enable him to make of himself whatever he thinks of himself as being, to become whatever he wishes to become, to transform his soul in perfect accord with whatever ideal he may have for that soul. In these lessons we have indeed given unto you the Science of Self-regenerating and self-transformation, by which you may become whatever you will to become. By the application of this Science, every one may become a Jehovah, or Yahwah, and I will be what I will to be. Thought is the instrument with which you are to transform your soul, your life and even your body into the image of that which you think. Truly you are whatever you think, "as a man thinketh in his heart, so is he." Let this, therefore, suffice concerning the Science of Alchemy.